Reforming Regulation

A Conference Sponsored by the
American Enterprise Institute for Public Policy Research
and the National Journal

Reforming Regulation

Edited by
Timothy B. Clark, Marvin H. Kosters, and James C. Miller III

American Enterprise Institute for Public Policy Research
Washington and London

Library of Congress Cataloging in Publication Data

Main entry under title:

Reforming regulation.

    (AEI symposia ; 80D)
    1. Independent regulatory commissions—United
States—Congresses. 2. Administrative law—
United States—Congresses. 3. Trade regulation—
United States—Congresses. I. Clark, Timothy B.
II. Kosters, Marvin H. III. Miller, James
Clifford. IV. American Enterprise Institute for
Public Policy Research. V. National journal.
VI. Series: American Enterprise Institute for
Public Policy Research. AEI symposia ; 80D.
KF5407.A5R42   342.73   80–21804
ISBN 0–8447–2189–1
ISBN 0–8447–2188–3 (pbk.)

AEI Symposia 80D

Printed in the United States of America

Participants

Dennis Avery
Special Assistant
Commodities Futures Trading Commission

Elizabeth E. Bailey
Member, Civil Aeronautics Board

William J. Baroody, Jr.
President, American Enterprise Institute

Stephen G. Breyer
Chief Counsel, Senate Judiciary Committee

Clarence J. Brown
United States Congressman

Timothy B. Clark
Correspondent, *National Journal*

Richard E. Cohen
Correspondent, *National Journal*

Douglas M. Costle
Administrator, Environmental Protection Agency

Robert W. Crandall
Senior Fellow, Brookings Institution

Lloyd N. Cutler
Counsel to the President

John T. Dunlop
Professor of Economics, Harvard University

George C. Eads
Member, Council of Economic Advisers

Wayne G. Granquist
Associate Director
Office of Management and Budget

Mark J. Green
Director, Congress Watch

Contents

PART SIX
COST-BENEFIT ANALYSIS OF SOCIAL REGULATION

PART SEVEN
THE ADMINISTRATION'S REGULATORY REFORM INITIATIVES

PART EIGHT
OVERVIEW AND SUMMARY

Foreword

William J. Baroody, Jr.
and
John Fox Sullivan

"Our statute books are filled year after year with crude social and industrial experiments based upon no careful analysis or tabulated experience, and our civil service has only just begun to grope after intelligent standards." We cannot claim that comment as our own. It was said almost seventy years ago by Henry L. Stimson. Mr. Stimson, a good Progressive and a friend and adviser to Teddy Roosevelt, decried the inefficiency and confusion in government regulation before the First World War. He expressed great optimism, however, about the potential for improving regulatory techniques—for devising regulatory legislation and administration on a "scientific" basis. Somehow, that era of "scientific" standards he saw just beginning then has been just beginning for a long time.

After decades of intermittent enthusiasm for regulatory reform, what has changed the most, perhaps, is that reformers no longer tout their proposals as "scientific." The public is no longer so enthralled with "scientific experts." We have few illusions by now that the experts will somehow come up with that perfect formula, that ultimate principle or technique, that will allow us to go home and leave the tough decisions to the regulators with perfect confidence in their conduct. Up to a point, it is surely a good thing for us to recognize that deliberation about regulatory policies or procedures can never be entirely separated from the rough-and-tumble of everyday politics. Leaving things entirely to the experts would be confessing our exhaustion with the enterprise of self-government.

Still, we must beware of lowering the debate by resort to the righteous rhetoric or emotional sloganeering that is too often characteristic of contemporary politics. The danger is not simply that an overcharged atmosphere will lead us to make foolish or impulsive decisions. The more insidious danger is that in such a climate we will lose sight of what is actually being decided. Both the American Enterprise Institute and the *National Journal* are committed to the principle that public policy decisions can be improved through "the competition of ideas," but we are quite aware that ideas do not compete fairly in the political marketplace if they are packaged in deceptive rhetoric or pressed on the public through slogans that intimidate more than illuminate. Serious questions inevitably provoke serious disagreements, but debate can only be productive if it is focused on genuine issues. A debate among scarecrows serves only the magpies.

It is in that spirit that we have organized this conference on regulatory reform. We do not aim at establishing a final consensus on *the* problem with federal regulation: that would inevitably force us to resort to platitudes so broad and vague that quite divergent critiques could shelter under them with equal comfort. We do not aim to achieve complete agreement on the appropriate remedies: that would force us to settle on a lowest common denominator of reform proposals, on changes so innocent that they would offend no one. Rather, we have gone out of our way at this conference to ensure that our participants would be men and women of conviction as well as experience. We have tried to structure their contributions around specific proposals, to keep the debate here as carefully focused as possible.

We hope that this conference, if it does not radically change our thinking, will sharpen our perceptions of the central issues in the debate. The active involvement here of regulators and policy makers may enable them to address problems with greater insight and more precision in the future. The ultimate course of the debate on regulation is crucial because it is, in the last analysis, a debate about the way we are to be governed in this country.

Introduction

Timothy B. Clark, Marvin H. Kosters, and
James C. Miller III

The decade of the 1970s witnessed a surge of regulatory initiatives unprecedented in the history of the United States and then, ironically, a surge of second thoughts about the wisdom of those endeavors.

Had we gone too far? Had our best intentions got the better of us? Had idealism reached beyond the bounds of practicality? Could we afford to pay for the cleanest air and water, the safest workplaces and products, racial and sexual employment quotas regardless of merit, energy so cheap as to discourage self-sufficiency?

Was the cumulative effect of government intervention in the private sector damaging the free enterprise spirit that built the most productive economy in the world? And if so, what could be done to bring into balance the goals of the government's regulatory enterprise and the age-old ideals of freedom and productivity in the United States?

These were among the questions addressed by a distinguished group of government and private speakers at a May 1979 conference—"Regulatory Reform: Striking a Balance"—sponsored by the American Enterprise Institute for Public Policy Research and the *National Journal.* As we enter the 1980s, these questions will be among the principal subjects of debate in our society.

Scholars and members of Congress argued in the late 1970s that regulation was becoming as important a technique of governing society and redistributing income as direct spending in the public sector. Although the federal budget, when it broke the half-trillion-dollar mark, was still roughly five times as great as the cost of regulation, regulation was gaining fast. Murray L. Weidenbaum of AEI and others argued that regulation cost more than $100 billion in 1979.

The effects of regulation were felt by individual citizens across the land. Traffic control programs in major cities, designed to clean up air pollution, were stalled for lack of citizen support. Detroit's efforts to meet conflicting federal mandates to reduce pollution, build safer cars, and increase mileage made its products more expensive. As companies closed factories because it was uneconomic to meet pollution or safety goals or they could not compete with the cheaper products of less strictly regulated foreign firms, the public protest against regulation grew. The passage of Proposition 13 in California in 1978 and tax limitation measures in other states helped convince politicians that the people wanted less government, including less regulation.

Yet while surveys showed people angry about the general idea of regulation, they also showed that the public wanted more, not less, regulation to achieve such specific goals as a cleaner environment and safer products. And press coverage of disasters on the James River and at Love Canal led to demands for stricter controls on industry.

By 1979, however, many in government, including the president, believed that regulatory programs were often inefficient and imposed an unnecessary drag on the economy. The central question was how to improve their performance without unduly impeding progress toward goals still deemed worthy.

There were no easy solutions. It took the Occupational Safety and Health Administration more than a year to eliminate some 900 nit-picking rules nearly everyone agreed were unneeded. Deregulation of the airlines, begun by administrative action and speeded by legislation, took longer, even though the arguments that both airlines and passengers would benefit have proved to be true.

These two examples illustrate a greater difficulty in the path of regulatory reform. The programs administered by the OSHA and the Civil Aeronautics Board do not have much in common, nor do the programs of the Environmental Protection Agency, the Interstate Commerce Commission, and the Commodity Futures Trading Commission. Each is authorized by a separate statute designed to deal with a distinct set of problems. And that, of course, means that no single statute Congress might enact can "reform" all the agencies. The government-wide regulatory reforms advocated by the administration and some members of Congress—and discussed at the AEI-*National Journal* conference—dealt with procedural issues, not with the substance of the laws underlying the regulatory schemes that industry and others have felt so burdensome.

One panel at the conference discussed case-by-case reform of economic regulatory agencies—those created to control entry and price in industries where natural monopolies were thought to exist or where competition was thought to be harmful to the national interest. The most prominent example was the airline industry, in which deregulation appeared to be benefiting nearly all concerned. Deregulation, clearly the most radical of possible reforms, has also been proposed—and partially implemented by administrative action—in trucking, banking, rail transport, and communications. In the banking industry, legislation enacted in March 1980 is designed to promote considerably increased competition among financial institutions. Deregulation has not come quickly, for the industries affected have generally resisted. The trucking industry, for example, put up a powerful fight that had trucking deregulation stalled on Capitol Hill in the spring of 1980 even though proponents of the legislation claimed it could save consumers billions of dollars a year.

While the administration and consumer groups were behind the moves to reduce economic regulation, they fought hard against industry attempts to escape from "social" regulation of the kind performed by the OSHA, the Federal Trade Commission, and the Environmental Protection Agency. Used car dealers, funeral parlor operators, and television advertising interests were among those that sought, with limited success, to curtail the powers of the FTC in 1979 and 1980. In the fall of 1979, strip mining companies persuaded the Senate to overturn Interior Department rules they said were too costly, although the House did not go along. In the spring of 1980, public transit operators seemed on their way to gaining congressional approval of a measure to throw out Transportation Department regulations that would force them to spend billions of dollars to serve wheelchair users.

But such case-by-case forays against individual regulatory problems could not be counted on to succeed. Indeed, there were more failures than successes. So a search continued in 1979 and 1980 for some more generalized approach that could reform the regulators—force them to minimize the inflationary impact of their rules.

Process was the watchword. If somehow the agencies could be made to follow new procedures in formulating their regulations, perhaps the substance of those regulations would be less burdensome. Some advocates of procedural reforms maintained that the agencies could never reform themselves and that the president, Congress, or the courts should be given more power to review and overturn agency rules. Proposals for procedural reform provided the only focal point in the debate about overregulation, and they were the subject of most of the panels at the AEI-*National Journal* conference.

A group of top officials of the Carter administration described their efforts to gain better control of regulation and the legislation the president had proposed to strengthen those endeavors. In March 1978, building on programs instituted by his predecessor, the president issued Executive Order 12044, which requires agencies to:

- analyze the costs and benefits of major proposed regulations and give good reasons if they choose options other than the least expensive

3

- ensure that their top officials supervise the regulation-writing process
- provide increased opportunity for public participation in the process
- review existing regulations regularly and weed out those that are outdated
- write their rules in plain English

A key feature of the scheme that has provoked much controversy was the requirement for better economic analysis of proposed rules. The administration characterized the requirement as "regulatory analysis," shying away from the term "cost-benefit analysis," although that was clearly behind the idea. Labor unions and environmental, consumer, and other "public interest" groups strenuously resist the notion that agencies should be forced to submit their actions to a cost-benefit test. They contend, not without reason, that while costs can be measured with a degree of accuracy, benefits are not so easily measurable. A cost-benefit requirement, they fear, would focus attention on costs without commensurate attention to relatively unquantifiable benefits. One of the conference panels debated this question.

Measurement of regulatory costs would be taken several steps further if, as members of another panel proposed, the administration developed a regulatory budget. The idea was to decide each year how great a regulatory burden the government should impose on the private sector. Once a ceiling was established, a limit would be placed on the activities of each regulatory agency. Although this idea has practical difficulties, it is attractive to economists and other scholars. But it is anathema to interests supporting greater regulatory endeavors, as consumer advocate Ralph Nader made plain during the panel discussion of the regulatory budget.

Cost-benefit analysis and even the regulatory budget are ideas that seek to give the executive branch more power to manage the regulatory process. But some members of Congress believe that their branch of government should play an even greater role.

Senator Charles H. Percy of Illinois has advocated enactment of "sunset" legislation that would force Congress to review the charters of regulatory agencies on a set schedule; if the agencies were not granted new authorizing legislation, they would go out of business. At a panel on the sunset idea, Senator Percy described the legislation he has introduced. In a separate, major speech, Senate Judiciary Committee Chairman Edward M. Kennedy advocated a variation on the theme, the "high noon" provisions of his own regulatory reform legislation. "Public interest" groups again opposed the sunset proposal, fearing that it would lead to scaling back regulatory programs they support.

A more radical proposal for day-to-day involvement of Congress in the affairs of the regulators is that of Congressman Elliott H. Levitas of Georgia, Senator Harrison H. ("Jack") Schmitt of New Mexico, and others for a legislative veto of proposed regulations. The strongest of the legislative veto proposals would allow either the House or the Senate to set aside any regulation promulgated by an agency. The administration and most liberal interest groups have fought the idea, on the grounds that it may well violate the Constitution and that it would impose an impossible workload on Congress. Both Congressman Levitas and Senator Schmitt argued for their idea during a panel discussion on the topic.

Others believe that the judicial branch of government should play a greater role in overseeing the regulatory agencies. In September 1979 Senator Dale Bumpers of Arkansas successfully sponsored a Senate amendment that would remove the presumption that an agency rule is valid and thus give challengers a much-enhanced opportunity to make their cases in court. The administration and various defenders of regulation attacked the amendment. The administration argued that its regulatory reform efforts were designed to make the agencies more accountable to elected authorities and that to give power over agency rules to judges appointed for life was hardly increasing accountability in the regulatory process.

As this volume went to press, all these questions were very much under debate. The administration's regulatory reform legislation, wending its way through the House and Senate judiciary committees and the Senate Governmental Affairs Committee, was developing into a vehicle for resolving many of them. But it seemed entirely possible that the debate could carry on to the 97th Congress, since the administration was threatening to veto a bill containing the legislative veto provision, the Bumpers amendment, or other stringent curbs on regulation that were increasingly popular on Capitol Hill.

Part
One

Perspectives on Regulation and Its
Reform

Overview of Regulatory Effects and Reform Prospects

Paul W. MacAvoy

Government intervention in American commerce dates from colonial times, but industry-specific regulation began just over ninety years ago, with passage of the Act to Regulate Commerce (1887). Since then, and particularly since the 1930s, state and federal regulatory agencies have set the prices and certified the services of utilities and of companies that transport passengers and freight. Within the last two decades, regulatory controls have been extended to cover natural gas and petroleum products companies directly and health service organizations indirectly. Regulation has spread even further in the past few years as new agencies have been set up to control environmental quality and health and safety conditions in workplaces throughout the economy.

As regulation has expanded, so has the movement for deregulation. Recent proposals for regulatory reform have gone beyond simply calling for improved agency procedures. The Ford administration proposed legislation to eliminate federal price-setting authority over railroads, airlines, trucking companies, banking institutions, and gas producers. These initiatives did not succeed, but during the Carter administration airline passenger fares and natural gas prices were to be deregulated in phases over the early 1980s. Both administrations made extensive efforts to reorganize agency activities or constrain agency decisions so as to reduce the scope of existing regulation.

Although reform of the regulatory commissions had been tried before, the Ford and Carter initiatives were both more comprehensive and more fundamental. For the first time, they sought to restrict regulation per se, rather than to adjust or limit some agency prerogatives. These proposals to deregulate took the form of legislative as well as administrative changes.

Proponents of the new approach argue that regulation has not produced the desired results. They assert that the rapid extension of new

---

This paper draws heavily, with the permission of the publisher, on *The Regulated Industries and the Economy*, by Paul W. MacAvoy (W. W. Norton & Co., 1979), which contains detailed documentation of the results summarized here.

9

health and safety regulations has increased industry costs while the benefits have fallen far short of the statutory goals of creating a safe and clean economy. They also assert that regulation of public utilities has adversely affected the service and growth of those and other industries. These critically important assertions are reviewed and evaluated in this essay.

Whether regulation has in fact had such effects can partially be determined by looking at prices and service offerings in the transportation and public utilities industries and in the manufacturing industries most subject to safety, health, and environmental regulations. An examination of growth in output and price changes can indicate how well the regulated sectors of the economy have functioned. The results of such an examination strongly suggest that these industries have done less well than others in ways that are attributable to regulation.

The Characteristics and Growth of Regulation

Traditional regulation has centered on controlling prices and entry of companies in interstate transportation (railroads and trucking firms), communications (telephones and broadcasting), electricity production, and pipeline transportation (natural gas pipeline companies). In most of these industries, prices have been kept down by commission or agency review in courtlike proceedings of company requests for revenue increases. Both state and federal commissions have also set price differences for varying types of service and entry conditions into most or all markets. They have monitored service quality and extended service coverage to new communities, customers, and conveniences.

From the beginning the regulatory agencies were justified on the grounds that without controls firms in these particular industries would not sufficiently improve the quality or increase the volume of service. The companies with monopoly power would set prices too high and would not provide service to outlying regions and infrequent users that required them to extend existing systems. To achieve the greatest commercially feasible extension of service systems, regulation had to keep the company from monopoly pricing and also to allow it to charge higher-than-competitive prices on some services to subsidize growth in others. The justifications used to initiate controls were subsequently invoked to extend them through the 1970s. The rationales of lower price and improved service were invoked in support of regulation of natural gas prices, crude oil and products prices, trucking and airlines, and the communications industry.

Regulation was not limited to price control and service enhancement but included early attempts to improve health, safety, and working conditions as well. Particularly important initiatives included the Food and Drug Administration, established in 1931, and the Federal Aviation Administration, begun in 1948. They served as models for setting standards to improve product or service safety. Most of the federal agencies responsible for setting performance standards, however, have been established in the last ten years. Two of the most significant are the Environmental Protection Agency and the Occupational Safety and Health Administration. Both have affected conditions in almost every industry. The agency having the most comprehensive authority in a single industry is the National Highway Traffic Safety Administration, which sets performance standards for automobiles.

Regulation has been justified primarily on the grounds that private producers fail to take into account the social harm of unhealthy and unsafe conditions of production. The rationale is that since excessive harm follows from ignoring social costs, activities entailing excessive social costs should be controlled. But the goals set in the enabling legislation for these agencies make it evident that the adverse conditions are to be eliminated as long as it is technically feasible to do so.

A number of agencies administer a broad range of controls that account for federal administrative expenditures of slightly more than $3 billion per year. This figure alone is not indicative of regulation's full impact on economic activity, however. A few dollars spent on regulatory activity can initiate large costs in a substantial share of private-sector industry and trade. The effective coverage of controls is indicated by accumulating, industry by industry, the share of national output produced by industries falling under government regulation (as in table 1). The public utilities and transportation companies, under the jurisdiction of price-regulating commissions, account for somewhat more than 5 percent of total gross national product (GNP). When the regulatory process was extended to petroleum production, refining, and marketing in the mid-1970s, another 3 percent of GNP was brought under agency surveillance. The financial sector, which accounts for approximately 3 percent of GNP, typically has had either national or state controls on entry, service offerings, and interest rates.

The most significant new regulatory coverage of the economy occurred with the establishment of agencies to increase workers' health and safety (OSHA) and to protect the environment (EPA). Their controls cover virtually every manufacturer. In practice, however, a few industries were more significantly affected than others to the point of adjusting their pricing, production, and investment decisions. A large percentage of the investments of the mining, construction, and chemical industries was diverted to meet regulatory requirements for equipment. The paper, primary metal, motor vehicle, stone, clay, and glass product,

11

TABLE 1

Percentage of GNP in the Regulated Sector of the Economy

Category	Percentage of GNP under Regulation in 1965[a]	Percentage of GNP under Regulation in 1975[a]
Price regulation[b]	5.5	8.8
Financial markets regulation[c]	2.7	3.0
Health and safety regulation[d]	—	11.9
Total	8.2	23.7

[a] The calculations are GNP originated by industry group as a percentage of GNP originated by all industry. Industries are defined as including those companies or activities accounted for in the Department of Commerce Standard Industrial Classification (SIC).
[b] Includes railroads (40), motor freight transportation and warehousing (42), air transportation (45), communications (48), electric, gas, and sanitary services (49), and (for 1975 only) crude petroleum and natural gas (13) (SIC codes in parentheses).
[c] Includes banking (60) and insurance (63) (SIC codes in parentheses).
[d] Includes metal mining (10), coal mining (11–12), mining and quarrying of nonmetallic minerals (14), construction (15–17), paper and allied products (26), chemical and allied products (28), petroleum and related industries (29), stone, clay, and glass products (32), primary metal industries (33), motor vehicles and equipment (371) (SIC codes in parentheses).
Source: U.S. Department of Commerce, *Workfile* 1205–02–02, 1976 revision.

and petroleum refining industries did not have to make quite as extensive investments in plant and equipment, but controls were placed on key production processes or products through specific work-safety rules and pollution-emission restrictions. These industries together account for almost 12 percent of GNP. The regulated sector of the economy at the end of the 1970s thus produced nearly 24 percent of GNP (as shown in table 1). This percentage is large enough at least to raise questions about whether we have a "regulated economy" and whether controls have been extended to too many private-sector activities. Before dealing with such questions, however, one must determine how these agencies operate.

The Regulatory Process

What do these regulatory agencies actually do and with what result? Although each agency begins with a different function, a uniformity of process can be observed that permits generalizations about performance. Each agency has political appointees as executives to make decisions, a permanent staff to administer the decisions, and substantial financial support to carry out its operations. Decisions and operations are supposed to carry out the mandate in the statute. As an agency develops, its procedures and decisions tend to resemble those of other agencies.

This happens in part because the various agencies, boards, and commissions use many of the same arguments and factual foundations. Although they consider a wide range of testimony and evidence, in practice they use a small set of physical and financial accounting measures of previous activities as the basis for decisions. In price-regulation cases, revenue increases are justified by changes in historical costs as shown in corporate accounting statements of income and assets. In health and safety regulations, controls on equipment are specified by engineering studies. In both, behavior in the present and the near future is constrained by recent past performance, which results in less change in the regulated industries than in other industries.

Two factors make for such operating results. First, the legislative mandates of different agencies have been similar, in some cases even being couched in the same language. The goals of the Act to Regulate Commerce of 1887—stabilizing prices, expanding service, and promoting equity in railroad fare structures—were repeated in later transportation regulatory statutes. To be sure, the commissions controlling health, safety, and environmental conditions were called on to solve different problems from those in the public utility industries, but similarities of language within health and safety mandates brought about similar processes and criteria for setting standards in agencies of that kind.

The second factor has been the Administrative Procedures Act and its recourse to court review. This general law sets requirements for open hearings, presentation of evidence, and justification of case decisions in most of the agencies. By allowing the courts to review the agency's decisions to ensure the access of interested parties and due consideration by the agency of the evidence presented, the act naturally leads to greater use of quantitative than of judgmental or predictive materials. The courtlike proceedings under the act emphasize evidence on existing conditions and thereby take less account of possible future gains or losses from alternative conditions. The scope of judicial review has encompassed not only whether a statute is being complied with but whether the procedures chosen by the agencies are "reasonable." To avoid unfavorable review on these issues, the agencies establish more procedural conformity.

The case process itself sets limits on price or rate increases in the public utility and transportation industries. The agencies hold increased rates to the sum of operating costs in recent periods, depreciation, taxes, and a "reasonable profit." The profit estimates are arrived at by applying a "reasonable" rate of return to the capital rate base. Once the agency has concluded what total expenses and profit should be, the company sets prices so as to produce revenues no greater than this allowance. Judgmental elements play a role, particularly in determining the reasonable rate of return, but there has been a tendency for estimates of the rate to lie within a narrow range. The results in price-control agencies have therefore been similar across cases and over time.

The agencies regulating health and safety conditions have also developed a common process. After prolonged adversary proceedings, they have focused on quantitative specifications of equipment and plant operating conditions. These specifications are easier to certify and enforce than other kinds of standards. They are designed for indirect control of the company's performance on health conditions, operating safety, and environmental quality. In important instances, however, the standards, rather than their actual health or environmental effects, have become the primary focus of decision making.

The Effects of Regulatory Growth

The spread of regulation is another part of the story. The major concerns are how the commissions have operated and how companies have fared under controls. Some regulated firms and some entire regulated industries have performed well relative to the economy as a whole, but others have not done as well as they might have without controls. In general, economic and political conditions in the last ten years have been such that price and safety regulations have not been able to produce the desired results. Regulation has not added to economy-wide efficiency and growth, as it would if prices and service expansion had been in keeping with the original goals. In health and safety regulation, the costly equipment standards have not achieved improved working and living conditions.

This may have been the product of chance or design. But in fact the particular practices worked out through case-by-case decision making were particularly unproductive in the economic conditions of the 1970s. During the inflation of the late 1960s and early 1970s, agency-allowed annual percentage price increases were smaller and output growth was larger than in industries not subject to price controls. That is, average annual rates of price increase in the regulated utilities lagged behind those found elsewhere, creating a significant impetus for more rapid growth in demands for regulated services.

The increased demands could be satisfied only so long as there was additional capacity to expand production. Reduced growth in capacity by the middle and late 1970s reduced the growth rate of production in relation to unregulated industries more than could be attributed to the business cycle. Although some catchup in price increases occurred in the middle 1970s, recessionary conditions during that period put price increases out of phase. By the end of the decade, these regulated industries, rather than leading in investment and production, lagged behind the rest of the economy.

At the same time, the half-dozen industries most subject to health, safety, and environmental controls began to show the effects of regulation. Price increases were larger and output increases smaller than elsewhere, as if regulation had begun to make production more costly. This was not contrary to the goals of regulation, however. Given the mandate to eliminate social harms wherever found, health and safety regulation *should* have reduced both the capacity and the production of polluters and unsafe producers, thereby increasing costs of final goods and services. But this regulation should also have provided improved health and cleaner air. Instead, health and safety controls operated in the 1970s without substantial benefit to the quality of working conditions or of the environment.

Two distinct regulatory processes contributed to these results. Regulatory lag began to work against rather than for these companies, and the regulatory agencies restrained current-dollar rate increases. Before the mid-1960s, when costs were falling but rates were kept constant, regulatory lag was to the advantage of the regulated firm because profits continued to increase until the agency forced service increases or reductions in rates. When costs began to rise more rapidly, however, regulatory lag worked against the firm since its historical costs were below current costs. The difference between historical and current costs widened as the increase in rate applications extended the amount of time required for decisions. Thus, the greater the inflation and the longer the lag in allowing price increases, the greater the profit-reducing effects of controls.

Rate increases, when they were granted, were also smaller than those previously granted in relation to cost increases. The dollar size of the rate increases applied for was often very large, and out of concern for adverse public reaction, regulators became reluctant to grant even increases that were fully justified by the cost-based criteria that had previously been acceptable. In the transportation and electricity-producing sectors, where large fuel price increases were passed through automatically, rate increases to cover capital and operating cost increases were held down severely through the early and middle 1970s.

Since price changes did not fully compensate for cost increases, additions to capacity were curtailed, and the growth of production in the regulated industries fell below that in the rest of the economy.

15

Regulated companies became reluctant to introduce new services and were much slower to improve existing service. The constraints on growth in the energy, transportation, and communication industries in the 1970s had effects similar to the shortages caused by price controls in the natural gas industry, if not to the same degree.

While growth in industries subject to price and entry regulation was slowing as described, other industries found themselves subject to increasingly stringent safety and environmental controls. These industries also experienced greater reductions in output growth during the 1970s than other industries in the economy. But these regulatory results followed from moving not back down the supply function, but rather up the demand function. Faced with the price increases necessary to compensate for the cost increases required to meet standards, the growth of demand was reduced. The producers were not much affected—for the most part, profit margins were not reduced in the industries affected by health, safety, and environmental regulations in comparison to other industries. The higher costs attributable to regulation were largely passed on to consumers, while the quality of life was not improved. Evaluations of the effects of the EPA, the NHTSA, and the OSHA are subject to great imprecision because of errors in measuring performance in relation to what might have occurred in the absence of regulation, but the evidence suggests that national equipment standards provided no significant improvements through the middle 1970s. Again, as in the case of price regulations, these results have not occurred by chance, nor have they been the design of policy makers; rather they have followed necessarily from the regulatory process.

To bring about any improvement, the process must be changed. The control system must allow prices of the regulated companies to respond to changes in cost and demand. Regulation to improve health, safety, and environmental quality must replace equipment specifications with cost-effective and beneficial performance standards.

How to Reform Price Regulation

The regulatory process has come under great pressure for change in day-to-day case hearings, in appeals of decisions in the courts, and in the legislature. In response to this pressure, considerable change in administrative practice has occurred; new rule makings have replaced or accelerated the flow of case decisions and, more important, new standards established for case decisions on revenue increases have relaxed the previously severe limits on those increases.

The most widespread means of effecting this change has been a general relaxation of the old rate-base standards in revenue request

16

cases. There have been two approaches: (1) before the case is decided, to allow more temporary rate increases, and (2) after the case is decided, to allow a higher rate of return.

There has also been some legislative change. In the late 1970s, Congress mandated decontrol of railroad rates, airline passenger fares, and natural gas field prices. The important first step, however, had been initiated by the agency before statutory changes. All three industries had been operating under increasingly stringent price controls and were consequently finding it hard to adjust to increased demands, given the high inflation throughout the economy. To deal with this, the agencies themselves promoted limited internal deregulation. The adjustments in air fares showed that flexibility and increased variability in fares did not result in disruption of service.

Since natural gas regulation had been much more restrictive than airline regulation, gas markets had further to go to achieve market equilibrium. The use of "phased" deregulation to achieve an end to gas shortages was of necessity extremely complicated. In light of the large increase in consumer expenditures that would be implied by complete decontrol, Congress had to consider not only the positive effect of reducing shortages but also the adverse political impact on lawmakers of substantial price increases to current residential and commercial users. But the Federal Power Commission paved the way by tripling the basic allowed price on new gas in 1976 without widespread consumer revolt.

These examples indicate the important role commission initiatives played in phasing out regulation. By selectively decontrolling certain aspects of behavior, the sudden impact of a shift to open markets was reduced. Congress merely followed the path set by the agencies. The issue raised by phased reductions in controls is whether the process really does result in fully deregulated markets. Regulation has been prolonged and in the gas case extended beyond markets regulated earlier. If prices at the end of the phasing are still too low, the transition will most likely continue so as to make regulation and phased decontrol indistinguishable.

How to Reform Health and Safety Regulation

Certain changes in internal review processes could substantially improve the results of controls in the new agencies. The most important of these would require some assessment of the results of regulation as part of the formulation of new standards. The Ford and Carter administrations both proposed that major rule makings be justified by findings that the new rules would produce economy-wide gains. Any new rule also had to prove less costly than alternative regulatory policies. Since 1975 such regulatory agencies as the EPA, the OSHA, and the NHTSA have been making such findings on economy-wide impact as part of their rule making.

In theory, this new process should reduce or even eliminate excessive regulation. The impact statement that reveals adverse economy-wide results should stand in the way of the issuance of excessive standards. There is a vast difference, however, between the best possible results of invoking such a policy and its practical effects. The impact statement has not been required of all federal agencies; the independent regulatory commissions were exempt, for instance. In practice, the implementation of these procedures was limited to half a dozen agencies in the Office of the President. More showed adverse effects since the statements served as part of the justification process after decisions had been made rather than as part of the work preparatory to making decisions.

But the process could go one step further by allowing all parties to make such analyses and requiring the agency to exercise "reasonable" choice among contradictory findings. This would compel agencies to take account of the economy-wide effects of their rules. Such impact statements would hinder further development of ineffective and costly equipment standards, even though they have not yet been sufficiently incorporated into decision making to make regulation generally more effective.

Reform by Court Decree

Recent court decisions evaluating the health and safety control process are an important new element in this regulation. In the first stages of this regulation, the courts, on appeal of agency rule makings, were willing only to determine the fairness of proceedings and whether there was factual support for agency conclusions in the records of the proceedings. This approach encouraged the building of lengthy dockets on equipment specifications, but it did not significantly affect the results of the rule-making process. In five recent occupational and highway safety cases, however, the federal judiciary, at least tentatively, began to evaluate the results of rule making.

These case decisions both directed the agencies away from rule making requiring equipment on feasibility grounds alone to standards justified on the grounds that the total economic and social performance of the regulated companies would be improved under the new regulations. Those aspects of performance would include accident reduction, improvement in health, and greater product quality. Whether such changes could be translated into economic benefits is problematic, but estimating the extent to which lives would be saved or products rendered more useful would still greatly improve the regulatory decision-making process. By adopting the courts' line of reasoning, these agencies could reduce the high-cost, low-benefit results of health and safety regulation.

Prospects for Reform

While the reform process has not been without accomplishments, the overall record falls short of what is needed to reverse recent declines in performance caused by controls in the regulated industries. Beyond regulatory lag and inefficiency, the poor results reflect the inevitable product of the present administrative procedures. The critical step toward improving the present condition of the regulated industries would be to develop new procedures in the agencies responsible for price controls and health and safety regulation.

Three kinds of changes are needed to transform given administrative procedures. The first would be to regulate prices by applying profit constraints based on current and future costs of capacity for providing service. The second would be to deregulate where conditions of competition, service quality, and the economy no longer justify ponderous and complicated control processes. The third would be to require that the effects of health and safety regulations be justified before rules are determined.

The question for the 1980s is whether it will be possible to reform regulation along these three lines. From all appearances, regardless of the abundance of reform rhetoric, the answer is that such changes are unlikely. The reason is that real regulatory change is impolitic—promising, as it does, transitional problems, less certain procedures and results, and losses to certain groups now benefiting superficially from too low prices or too much pollution control equipment.

In the 1980s the American economy will probably continue to operate under the regulatory legislation much as it now exists. As regulatory practices and rules expand, the agencies, boards, and commissions will reduce the returns on and the opportunities for capital and output growth. If inflation is extensive, the growth rates of the price-regulated industries will be reduced most. This effect will be seen in lower-quality service, slower expansion of service to outlying groups of consumers, and less introduction of technologically superior equipment and systems to those now receiving service. At the same time, the goods and services provided by the industries most affected by health, safety, and environmental regulation will be more expensive, less satisfactory in performance, and less likely to improve over time.

In short, prospects for significant reform of regulation do not appear favorable. But prospects would be enhanced by increased public understanding of the effects of our current regulatory process: a reduction in the performance of a number of important industries without the realization of many of the promised social benefits.

Regulatory Reform: Striking a Balance

Edward M. Kennedy

While examining regulatory reform, Senator John C. Culver, chairman of the Administrative Practice Subcommittee, received a letter from a constituent who was fed up with filling out forms instead of running his business. He had received an Equal Employment Opportunity Commission questionnaire that asked, "How many employees do you have, broken down by sex?" He wrote back: "None. Our problem here is alcohol."

My own concern with regulatory reform is not new. Neither is the country's. Regulation touches all of us because the cost of transportation and energy, the safety of food, drugs, jobs, and the quality of the environment are crucial to all of us. If Americans are to believe in their government, regulation must be—and must be seen to be—fair, reasonable, and effective.

In 1860 Ralph Waldo Emerson wrote that "the government, which was meant for protection and comfort of all good citizens, becomes the principal obstruction and nuisance; the cheat and bully we meet everywhere is the government." Twenty years later Congress created the Interstate Commerce Commission; a hundred years later we are trying to uncreate it. In the 1940s George Orwell articulated the terrifying vision of a government without limits, whose only constraint was that there were no more people or actions to dominate.

Since that time the growth of government has been explosive. Now we hear that regulation may cost the economy between $25 and $50 billion in paperwork alone; that the regulatory establishment grew 115 percent between 1975 and 1978, incurring annual budget costs of nearly $5 billion; that industry's regulatory compliance costs may be over $100 billion; that regulation may cost jobs, hit small business more heavily, be partly responsible for inflation, and at the same time be ineffective.

These costs do not mean that we can turn back the clock and return to the days of Ralph Waldo Emerson. Unlike Emerson, we live in a complex technological society where consumers have neither the knowledge nor the power to bargain for their interests.

Social regulation brings benefits, not just costs: clean air, a safe working place, promotion of minority employment, control of sickle-cell anemia, safe automobiles. The difficulty of measuring these benefits is no argument that they do not exist. It is a demonstration that cost-benefit analysis has limited utility in this sphere. That conclusion is inevitable because cost data come from interested businessmen whose accountants routinely tally them, while the public has no way and no incentive to tally the benefits. Thus, to pay too much attention to cost-benefit analysis or its brother, cost-effectiveness analysis, is to decide policy by relying on only one side of the ledger. That is unacceptable in a society that places a high premium on life, liberty, and the pursuit of happiness.

Nor do these costs of regulation mean that we should plunge head-long into deregulation in every area of governmental activity. The history of unregulated markets shows too clearly that they often prove detrimental to consumers and businesspeople alike. Recent revelations indicate that major asbestos firms were well aware of their product's harmful effects on workers and schoolchildren but covered up that knowledge for generations. The power company's behavior at Three Mile Island scarcely justifies a benign faith in the workings of the market. Complete decontrol of oil prices may well mean that the Invisible Hand belongs to a mugger instead of an agent for the general good.

The procedures of government clearly must be updated and re-vamped to achieve greater speed, openness, fairness, and efficiency, but procedural changes in regulation are unlikely to change its substantive results. Procedure alone will not give us lower prices, better health and safety, or a cleaner environment—and it is results that count.

Time has borne this out. For many years we thought agencies would regulate properly because they were merely transmission belts without power to make substantive policy, authorized only to apply Congress's orders to practical situations. It has become clear, however, that agencies are not just gear wheels; they make policy all the time. During the New Deal, we admitted this policy role but convinced ourselves that management by experts, controlled by basic precepts—"the science of the regulatory art"—would yield better results. This faith has been a snare and a delusion. There is no "science" of regulation; the proper allocation of rates, air routes, fuel oil, or protective respirators cannot be decided by abstract, neutral principles.

The procedural answer of the 1960s was to open the regulatory process—to provide more information to participants and to allow input from all potentially affected groups. We are still pursuing that effort—and more needs to be done—but such participation is seldom sufficient by itself to change regulation's basic course. This is not to say that increased procedural fairness, expertise, and participation are undesirable. To the contrary, they are critical in a democratic society. But we cannot count on procedure alone to produce major improvements in regulatory effectiveness.

How then are we to bring about meaningful change? I am convinced the key lies in agency-by-agency examinations of specific regulatory programs. Government bodies outside the agency concerned must take the time and effort needed to force change, and they need the help of outside groups committed to fundamental reform. In that work they should be guided by a philosophy of "regulation as a last resort." I would call this approach "least restrictive alternative" regulation.

That is the basic rule of our antitrust laws. Under those laws, when firms enter into an agreement, a court asks whether the agreement is necessary to achieve an important public purpose. The court allows the agreement only if it is "the least restrictive alternative" available to achieve that purpose.

This approach applies to government regulation, too. If we start out in favor of a competitive, unregulated marketplace, the government should intervene only when that market does not work properly—when it fails to fulfill an important public need. When the government does intervene, it should choose the least restrictive means available before turning to self-perpetuating commands and controls. At the very least, it should examine available alternatives in a regular, structured manner before choosing that route.

Practical consequences flow from this view. First, in the area of social regulation—traffic safety, food purity, drug efficacy, environmental protection, job safety and health—deregulation is unlikely to be an answer. There are too many powerful reasons—rooted in fairness, social justice, and relief for the disadvantaged and underrepresented—not to allow such regulation to be wiped away. We can never stop trying to make social regulation more effective and to incorporate new approaches, but past experience with unregulated drugs, pollution, and job conditions shows that relying on totally free markets here would invite chaos. Consumers do not have the knowledge or power to protect their best interests, and the protective efforts of more conscientious firms would be driven to the lowest common denominator. Here the choice will be how to regulate—not between regulation or none.

Second, where health and safety are not paramount and where industry consists of several firms in a reasonably competitive market, the most likely answer is not to regulate. Instead, we should rely on the discipline of that market, backed by antitrust policy. This has proved true for airlines. It also applies to trucking and other regulated industries. The best example is the Civil Aeronautics Board.

My Administrative Practice Subcommittee studied the CAB for

over eighteen months. We found that government regulation itself was the prime cause of high air fares. The CAB had effectively outlawed price competition, while channeling the airlines' competitive energies into excessive scheduling, gourmet meals, and other frills. The result was too many empty seats—for which ticket buyers paid.

Now airlines have been deregulated, and now they are charging lower fares and making more money. Demand has risen, and they are carrying more people to more places than ever before. In 1978:

- The real average domestic ticket price dropped nearly 10 percent, compared with the Consumer Price Index.
- Air customers saved over $2½ billion in fares.
- Carriers made record profits of $1.2 billion, for a 19 percent return on equity.
- The industry added 12,000 new jobs, including 1,100 in Boston alone.

This is how sensible deregulation can promote efficiency and reduce inflation at the same time.

Trucking is another patient that needs a healthy dose of competition. Since 1935 we have regulated trucks like trains. We have forced them to use listed routes, pretending they were like railroads whose huge investments in private track needed protection from wasteful competition. We have regulated their rates—not to keep them low, but to keep them high—to protect the monopoly value of their government licenses. We have even allowed them to set prices collusively—behind closed doors—in ways that are felonious in every other industry.

Trucks are not trains, and we should stop regulating as if they were. What is more, trucks are not public utilities. This is not a case where only a handful of firms can operate efficiently. The way to ensure fair truck rates—and lower prices for all consumers—is to unleash competition, not cage it more tightly.

Comprehensive legislation to reduce trucking regulation will soon be before Congress. I have already introduced S. 710, which would end legalized price fixing and limit the ICC's ability to outlaw competitive rates filed by carriers. This is an important step. Beyond it we must move to erase outmoded restrictions on entry, on mergers and acquisitions, and on other aspects of truck operations.

I believe we will succeed in this trucking effort. Many of our opponents in this fight for free enterprise are those who often urge less government intervention—for others, not themselves. Indeed, many members of the business community support regulatory reform, but always in someone else's area of business. With help from AEI and others, we can win this battle for the American people.

In other regulatory areas, however, the answer will not be to wipe the slate clean, but to make regulation less intrusive, less bumbling and bureaucratic. There are many tools the government can use to stop short of— or supplement—direct command-and-control regulation. The government can institute regulatory taxes. It can require more disclosure. It can encourage bargaining among private parties. The practical difficulties with these techniques should not be understated, but they may well make health, safety, and environmental regulation more effective and less cumbersome.

In the environment, for example, the goal is to encourage industry to use less polluting methods of production. Environmental taxes as supplements to direct standards have long been advocated by many environmentalists and by some in industry. The Environmental Protection Agency is currently experimenting with systems of "marketable rights" under which new firms can buy rights to pollute from older firms, creating a profit motive for both existing and new firms to reduce emissions in the most cost-effective ways. Regulatory taxes have been used to increase the price of throwaway cans and nonreturnable bottles, encouraging buyer shifts to more socially desirable products. They might also be used to regulate the price of cigarettes with dangerous levels of tar and nicotine or to raise the prices of automobiles with low gasoline efficiency.

We might also use increased disclosure to warn consumers away from products we do not want to forbid. We use mandated disclosure as a regulating technique in drug labeling, in food packaging, at the gas pump, in the stock market. It is less restrictive and sometimes more effective than banning a substance or product. As we discover that more and more necessary food substances also carry risks, we may want to require food labels warning consumers to eat what they want, but not too much of any one thing. Some have suggested a "dangerous food" area in each grocery store for products whose intake should be restricted, though not banned entirely. As a result of the saccharin mess, the Food and Drug Administration itself is exploring the possibility of regulating only "involuntary exposures" to food additives, not the hopeless task of regulating exposures that consumers with full knowledge still desire.

We might also make more use of informal bargaining to attain regulatory goals. In some European countries, workplace safety problems are negotiated among unions, management, and a government representative. Certain firms have quietly begun to work with the Occupational Safety and Health Administration to explore such techniques here. This process can take place on an informal, plant-by-plant basis, producing more effective regulation as well as freedom from unwieldy

25

requirements. It can also make direct government enforcement a matter of last resort rather than one of first instance.

Finally, in some areas it will not be possible to avoid direct regulation. Thalidomides must be banned. Nor would it be wise to rely solely on the marketplace for the purity of our air or drinking water. Effective regulation is as important to parents filling a prescription as to the workers who breathe the air in their plants. Government safety standards are equally important to the traveler in a plane and to the machinist at the workbench. There must be a Federal Aviation Administration, and there must also be direct government concern with worker safety. Reform here will be complex. It may involve giving agencies more resources or changing their procedures. It may involve increased enforcement or systems that encourage more voluntary compliance. It may also involve an admission that what works for General Foods is not right for the corner grocer.

In all these cases we can do more. We can encourage others to follow the same case-by-case approach and to do so by procompetitive means. We can legislate a system that will encourage scrutiny of individual agencies and require detailed reform plans. And we can promote regular examination of less restrictive alternatives to attain legitimate regulatory ends.

This week I will introduce legislation that adopts this substantive-reform approach. The bill has three basic objectives.

First, it will institutionalize substantive reform on a case-by-case basis, analyzing each agency by asking these questions:

- What is the market defect that justifies regulation by this agency?
- Are the methods used to correct this defect effective in achieving that goal?
- Are there less restrictive alternatives?

The bill contains a "high noon" provision which, by two trigger mechanisms, will expose a specific regulatory agency each year to the kind of piercing light that should uncover any defects.

The first trigger requires the president, along with a newly established Committee on Regulatory Evaluation—a committee with a fundamentally procompetitive outlook—to propose a regulatory reform bill and report dealing with one listed agency each year. Wherever possible, this report will review alternatives to direct regulation, evaluate procompetitive improvements, and favor consumers. The legislation mandates presidential review of ten categories of agencies in the decade between 1982 and 1992, including the ICC, the Federal Maritime Commission, the Federal Communications Commission, environmental agencies, and banking and financial regulatory agencies. Once in Congress, these reform proposals will be referred to the appropriate committee, which has 360 legislative days to consider the bill, amend it, and report it out.

Then comes the second trigger—a procedural trigger. If the committee does not act within a year, the bill can be discharged for privileged floor consideration. Thus, while it would still take two houses of Congress and the president to enact regulatory reform and the appropriate committees retain jurisdiction, this bill obviates the procedural tie-ups that frequently prevent Congress from getting to the heart of the matter.

The bill's second objective will focus on the daily substantive activities of regulatory agencies. Agencies concerned with economic regulation would be forced to consider whether their aims might be achieved through less restrictive alternatives and greater reliance on competition. This is an approach to reduced regulation that relies on agency, rather than congressional, initiative. This proposal will increase the use of competition as a regulatory tool. It targets the four types of federal regulatory activity that substitute direct economic regulation for the marketplace and that have historically had severe anticompetitive effects: limits on entry, control over prices, restraints on the amount of goods and services that may be produced or distributed, and approval of anticompetitive agreements among rival firms. An agency may regulate in these ways only after it has considered the effects of the action on competition and concluded that that action is the least anticompetitive alternative available to achieve its goals. Agencies may still regulate in the manner they deem necessary, but they would be required to consider competition to the maximum degree possible.

Third, the bill will increase the amount of meaningful public participation in agency rule making. This is critical not only for fairness but for improved agency decision making. The bill approaches this objective in four ways. It reforms the barebones "notice and comment" requirements for agency rule making and requires that rules having a major impact must give the public an increased opportunity to understand the arguments made and rebut them. It expands the kinds of rules that are subject to public participation by removing across-the-board exemptions for a number of agency functions presently immune from public scrutiny: the military, foreign policy functions, procurement, the giving of grants and benefits. It requires agency officials to log and summarize all communications made to them about a rule from persons outside the government after the proposed rule is published in the *Federal Register*. The bill also provides public participation funds for those persons and groups who will provide important points of view that should be taken into account in rule making. Finally, the bill improves the quality of agency procedures by setting up a committee in the Administrative Conference to create a uniform code of administrative procedures.

These provisions are consistent with the major regulatory reform bills now before the Senate, the Ribicoff bill and the administration's proposal. They complement and strengthen those bills. And they are consistent with what lies beneath those efforts—the widespread belief that there is too much costly and obtrusive government regulation, that Congress has created as many regulatory problems as it has solved, and that there is need for greater public participation in agency rule-making proceedings.

As we reach the 1980s, the issue of government credibility—its ability to respond sensibly and effectively, to know when to stay out as well as leap in—has grown larger. Our citizens and businesses feel overregulated. To most Americans regulation is not the president. It is not the secretary of energy or the Department of Health and Human Services. It is not even Washington. It is the energy allocation guidelines no one can understand. It is the government contract officer who puts people through hoops before looking at their applications. It is the inspector from the FAA or the OSHA or the Agriculture Department who may hold life-and-death power over their businesses but who does not seem to understand their operations and acts unwilling to learn. Striking the proper balance between compulsion and choice for individual citizens must be our focus. That is where gains must be made if we are to make a real difference. If faith in government's good sense, and even sanity, continues to decline, the will to respond where national response is truly needed will soon be gone, too.

The mainsprings of the current debate are the high cost of regulation, along with inflation, the general public feeling that government intervenes too much in our lives, and the breakdown of classical rationales for federal regulation. These are the reasons this subject has become more than the preserve of academics and commissions whose reports gather dust on Washington's bookshelves.

The answers to this debate will not be found in a return to the government of Franklin Roosevelt—but neither will they be found in a return to McKinley's. They will require new approaches and much hard work. That is something America has never been afraid of. Let us renew that fearless belief in new ideas. Let us strive together to make government work better for all the people.

Part
Two

Sunset Review

Introduction

W. S. Moore, Chairman

The sunset approach to regulatory reform is one of the more promising ideas to emerge during the 1970s. It has implications not only for the reform of regulation but also for reform throughout government.

Sunset is a relatively new term coined for a process that would change the way government has traditionally conducted its oversight and budgetary business. The prevailing assumption is that government agencies and programs continue unless there is a collective decision to stop one or more of them. This assumption makes a great deal of practical sense to the government because of the enormous effort required and the difficulty and cost involved in totally reevaluating each of its activities. Sunset would reverse the assumption so that each program to which it applies would automatically terminate unless there was a vote to continue it. Metaphorically speaking, the sun would set on these agencies unless the legislature took positive action to reestablish them.

Sunset, then, amounts to no more than a procedure for the legislature to follow, but it is a procedure that tips the scales the opposite way. It is always more likely that a legislature will fail to act rather than take a controversial step. Sunset shifts the burden of proof from those advocating termination to those advocating continuation. This shift in burden offers considerable promise to those seeking ways to manage the proliferation of government activities and to make them more effective. Sunset combines the complete-reevaluation feature of zero-based budgeting with an action-forcing mechanism—a deadline for automatic termination. The provision for automatic termination appears to have captured the imagination of reformers around the country. At least half the states have adopted some form of sunset legislation.

Why, given its promise and appeal, has the procedure not yet been attempted on a broad scale at the federal level? One reason is that there are at least three major practical, and to some degree conceptual, problems with designing and implementing a sunset procedure.

The first problem concerns the automatic termination feature. The virtue of automatic termination is that saving a program forces the

31

legislature to take action that legislatures have proved over time they are very reluctant to take. It forces a legislature to do a more thorough job of overseeing and evaluating the agencies and programs it has created and gives it a deadline by which it must act. The problem with automatic termination is that in many cases it is too extreme a remedy to be credible. The threat of major regulatory programs' being allowed to expire is simply not believable in this day and age.

Senator Percy, one of the principal advocates of sunset, proposes a modification of the action-forcing mechanism that may increase the probability of serious scrutiny and reform. This proposal would move toward automatic termination in three stages. If Congress takes no action to reestablish an agency by the first deadline, the agency's authority to issue new regulations would lapse. If Congress still has not acted by the second deadline, the agency's authority to enforce existing regulations would lapse. Failure to meet the third deadline would result in termination of the agency. While this modification is no panacea, its escalation of pressure on an existing program does offer Congress more options than merely a stark choice between sunset and business-as-usual and more time to consider the options in between. The procedure may well alter the political forces in certain cases and increase the prospects for constructive change.

The second major problem for sunset is the workload it entails. Complete reevaluation of all federal activities or even all regulatory programs is a mountainous task. That is why Senator Percy proposes to spread the evaluation of federal regulation over eight years. Mr. Avery makes very clear the size of the effort expended on just one agency—the Commodity Futures Trading Commission. Mr. Silberman proposes that the executive branch be required to evaluate and rank all its activities, including regulation, and report those rankings to Congress. While this might not ease the workload on the executive branch, it could make sunset manageable for Congress because the most likely serious candidates for sunset would tend to be those repeatedly ranked low by the executive branch.

It is necessary for sunset proposals to be exceedingly ambitious and practically all-inclusive to maintain the neutrality of the process. If certain agencies or programs were preselected for sunset review while others were exempted to reduce the workload, sunset would lose its neutrality and probably all chance of getting through Congress. Mr. Silberman's notion would strengthen sunset in the face of an impossibly large workload, though at the expense of acknowledged congressional dependence on the executive branch.

The third major problem is the central problem of sunset, underlying the two already mentioned. It involves the nature and strength of

32

the political forces generated by the review process and by practically any attempt to terminate a federal program. Mr. Avery gives a compelling description of the development and strength of the constituency against sunsetting the CFTC. His contention is that the strength of the constituency against termination (in Congress, in the agency itself, and in the private sector) is so much better placed and fights so much harder than any generalized reform constituency favoring termination of a particular agency or program that, on the basis of the CFTC experience, it is very unlikely that sunset will amount to much at the federal level. It is true that sunset is generally regarded as having failed in the case of the CFTC and the Consumer Product Safety Commission, but a similar process was successful in eliminating a number of federal advisory committees, and sunset has had some success at the state level.[1]

Mr. Silberman's and Senator Percy's proposals do offer a slight measure of optimism in response to Mr. Avery's experience and healthy pessimism. First, the senator's bill would establish an agenda for reform in which agencies and programs in related and overlapping areas could be compared with one another in the process of evaluation. Such comparisons may well strengthen constituencies for reform by moving the focus from a particular agency to a more general functional area of government. Second, Mr. Silberman's notion, which Senator Percy supports, of having government programs ranked according to effectiveness would produce public winners and losers among government activities. This, it is hoped, would energize the sleeping constituencies for reform in the press and among the general public that must be mobilized if the political forces Mr. Avery describes are ever to be defeated.

Sunset remains an idea of promise, not fulfillment. Perhaps modifications such as those suggested in this part will strengthen the sunset process enough to make its results worth the effort. Experience so far is not particularly encouraging, but one hopes that modifications based on a sophisticated appreciation of the drawbacks can make sunset a valuable tool for resolving one of the more intractable current problems of government. Perhaps a modified sunset in combination with the regulatory budget discussed in part four would provide some real hope for improving the effectiveness and accountability of government regulation.

---

[1] See D. Price, "Sunset Legislation in the United States," *Baylor Law Review,* vol. 30 (1978), pp. 401, 433–38.

Regulatory Sunset:
An Idea Whose Time Has Come

Charles H. Percy

The U.S. Chamber of Commerce, the Business Roundtable, the American Bar Association, and Common Cause have all endorsed regulatory sunset. The idea has to be either very good or terrible to draw a crowd like that. I hope the proposal has won such wide support because it is an idea whose time has come.

Regulatory sunset will have a great reception on the floors of the Senate and the House of Representatives. For the first time legislators have started to see what we in Congress—through statutes—and the regulatory agencies—through rules—have done to the rest of the country. Regulation has buried business, consumers, and state and local governments in mountains of paperwork. Congress is finally getting a taste of its own medicine, too, as it fulfills Federal Election Commission regulations for financial disclosure reports. Most important, we are beginning to realize that regulatory reporting and compliance cost money and we had better reevaluate them.

How much inflation today is attributable to regulation? Cost estimates are from $60 billion to $130 billion, depending on whose figures you take—in any case, a tremendous amount. Last year Congress freed the airlines, relatively speaking, from federal regulation. They are probably the only industry whose services in the last year have improved while prices dropped. Certainly, flights are more crowded, particularly in the center seat, but just look at prices: $107 now from coast to coast with no restrictions and $0.49 from Boston to Amsterdam if you want to stand in line for a week and a half. Despite those prices, airline profits have doubled. In a role reversal, the U.S. government is no longer subsidizing airlines but getting big revenues from them through the 46 percent corporate income tax. We need to combat inflation with other economic tools, too—balancing the budget, stimulating capital formation, providing incentives for productivity improvements—but regulatory reform can be a major factor in removing disincentives to capital formation and productivity.

The bill that I introduced in 1977, with Senator Robert Byrd and

Senator Abraham Ribicoff as principal cosponsors, and again this year as S. 445 with more than a third of the Senate cosponsoring, is a very simple concept. It requires that, in the first year of every new Congress, we review about one-fourth of the regulatory agencies. After eight years, Congress would have looked at each of the major agencies. Energy regulation would be one of the earliest, scheduled for the first year. In the first year also, by April 1, the president is required to present a reform plan on specified agencies, such as the Interstate Commerce Commission.

The ICC is a prime target for updating and modernizing. Our Rock Island Railroad in Illinois filed an application fifteen years ago to save itself from merging with the Union Pacific Railroad. Union Pacific wanted it because the Rock Island supplemented its routes, enabling it to provide much better service to the Midwest. For over eleven years there was ICC inaction and no decision, and the result was that the Rock Island went into bankruptcy.

Agency delays and regulatory indecisiveness are subject now to reform proposals of various kinds. One of these is S. 445 and the reform bill it requires the president to submit by April 1 in the first year of the session. By August 1 of the second session, if the appropriate committees and both houses of Congress have not taken action on the president's plan or one of their own, the named agency would lose the authority to issue new regulations—except essential health and safety rules. In other words, Congress would not immediately sunset the agency entirely. Rather, the first punitive measure would be to sunset the authority to issue new regulations. Therefore, lobbying groups that would ordinarily try to prevent legislation, such as truck deregulation, from being acted on, would have reason to urge action under S. 445 to save something from disappearing. If Congress still does not act by October 1, all authority to enforce existing regulation ceases, except in essential health and safety areas. And if, by the end of the session, December 31, no action has been taken by Congress, the agency itself is sunsetted—it goes out of business.

We anticipate that these punitive measures will never be required because we think Congress will act. Under budget reform (the Ervin-Percy-Muskie bill), we have mandatory dates by which Congress must act. We slipped a few days on the First Concurrent Resolution, but the discipline has still been tremendous. What we need for regulatory reform is discipline in a timetable, and that is why Senator Byrd's presence as a principal cosponsor is so important. He is not only majority leader but also a member of the Rules Committee, which has joined the Governmental Affairs Committee in drafting sunset.

What can we accomplish under our S. 445 mechanism? Obviously, one of the first things we are going to evaluate is energy regulation. Even though we have a new Department of Energy, all the old regulations still exist. It may be that Gary Seevers is against certain regulatory reforms and sunset. Yet I understand he could not attend this conference because he was in the Carolinas, dependent upon gasoline to drive back and unable to get enough. I share his consternation, because we both realize that the gasoline shortage today is a by-product of not allowing the free market to operate. Since costly new refinery capacity is needed to produce unleaded fuel, it is difficult today to buy that fuel.

It is regulation that has brought about this disparity of supply and demand. Refineries are ordered, for instance, to begin producing more heating oil in the height of the driving season, and this causes the panic of the "California syndrome." This and many other economic problems are the result of regulation—of escaping the action and the interaction of the free market. Getting rid of price controls in certain areas of the economy will let market forces operate. The longer we delay, the more painful the process will be.

In the case of natural gas for heating homes, regulation and price controls have caused Illinois and Washington, D.C., to be overdependent on this fuel. Why? Because the price is the lowest for the very best fuel when it ought to be the highest. We cannot convert to other means of heating as long as the best and the cleanest fuel is regulated to be the cheapest. That is not going to bring exploration and development of new supplies.

In light of all this regulation of energy, how do we achieve the president's goal of doubling coal production by 1985? As a member of the president's Coal Commission, I had to report to him recently that it is not possible. We are already a long way from that goal, and we are getting further from it now because a regulatory agency may require tighter air pollution standards that will provide a further disincentive for the use of coal. We are not asking for a change or a relaxation. We just do not want even tighter standards in this case because that would preclude the use of 40 to 70 percent of Illinois's coal in new coal-fueled power plants. One hand does not know what the other is doing. The regulatory agency is undercutting the president, as well as the Department of Energy. In the light of present circumstances, with no real health and safety standards involved, this proposed air standard makes no sense at all.

The time has come for regulatory reform. Its specific mechanism will be subject to a great deal of debate—and I am pleased that the American Enterprise Institute has joined with the *National Journal* to present this conference. The potential influence of the participants here in helping Congress to bring the reform process about is most encouraging to us on the Hill.

Extending Government Accountability to the Independent Agencies

Laurence H. Silberman

The key point that Senator Percy has made, which I would like to elaborate, is that our Constitution, our system, makes congressional action difficult, more difficult than in any other industrial democracy. The existence of two houses and the need for presidential acquiescence unless there is a two-thirds vote are evidence that the accretion of power was deliberately frustrated by the framers of the Constitution. It is always harder for Congress to act than not to act. The theory of sunset, of course, is to reverse the burden—to make it more difficult for Congress to ratify, to reaffirm, to reauthorize than it would be to repeal. This is a fundamentally sound notion because it accords with the basic structure of the Constitution.

However, I believe, that given the strength of what is popularly known as the iron triangle—relationships among committee staffs, the bureaucracy, and the constituency benefited by programs or regulation—it will be very difficult ever to eliminate portions of, let alone entire, programs or regulatory agencies. As I will explain, the Government Accountability Act, which Senator Percy and Congressman Sam Steiger introduced last year, focuses on programs rather than regulation in trying to strengthen the sunset concept. I want also to suggest that there may be a way to modify that proposal to make it even more valuable.

Underlying the Government Accountability Act is the notion that the problems of eliminating any government activity, regulatory or programmatic, include the lack of a common language of evaluation and the lack of press and public attention to the least effective programs. For these reasons, one cannot energize a constituency for reform that is capable of overriding the strength of those interested in a particular program's survival. Under the act the president would be required, once every two years, to report to Congress and, using various criteria, to rank the programs in a department in order of relative effectiveness. For example, if there are 200 programs in the Department of Health and Human Services, the president must rank them from 1 to 200 in order of relative effectiveness—and explain his ranking. For now, I am distinguishing the independent agencies from the regulatory programs that are parts of executive departments.

The independent agencies, though referred to in the act, are not part of the proposed structure. It would be possible, however, to require the president to rank the independent regulatory agencies from top to bottom in a separate package. Some independent agencies have several programs, but most of them have one, or perhaps two, major ones. It would be interesting if the president were forced to consider those agencies together and compare them with one another in relative effectiveness. The president does have some obligation, as the chief executive, to consider the impact of one independent regulatory agency in relation to all the rest, because it is clear that regulation is a seamless web as it applies to particular industries, to universities, and to other institutions. We might consider modifying the Government Accountability Act along these lines.

This leads me to a broader suggestion—something of a visionary notion. Last year, six of us went to the Virgin Islands to advise the governor on the adoption of a new constitution. Three of us were somewhat conservative Republicans, and three were Democrats, considerably more liberal. At one point in our discussions in a lovely cabana on the beach, the question was raised, What should we do with respect to independent regulatory agencies? Unanimously, we all said: "Make no provision for them. Preclude their existence." I thought about this response long and hard after that session, and I have concluded—forgive me for being revolutionary—that there is severe doubt about the propriety of having such agencies in this country. With their policy-making role and enormous power, these agencies are not subject to the political process in any meaningful way—even with sunset, even with the modifications I am suggesting. I have severe doubts whether Congress can really control an independent regulatory agency when it is outside the control of the president and therefore outside the control of the political process.

Some congressmen have considered this. Congressman Elliott Levitas of Georgia, for example, has suggested that Congress ought to pass on regulations as they come out. I am very dubious that that would work; it seems constitutionally strained, as well. Political control of the enormous policy-making responsibility of the independent regulatory agencies ought to be political in its broadest sense, not in the partisan sense.

Remember that our Constitution is designed to prevent easy accretion of power. This suggests that the very existence of the independent regulatory agencies is a device to get around the Constitution. To avoid the difficulty of accretion of power, the solution was to give a problem to a regulatory agency and let it develop rules that are really legislative in scope. I have reluctantly concluded that the only body in our society that has any possibility of coordinating the impact of the regulatory agencies is the judiciary, and clearly, in a policy sense, that is wrong: the judiciary should not be in that business. Yet there is no one else to do it.

The president has recognized that the activities of the independent regulatory agencies, as well as the regulatory agencies in the executive branch, have to be brought into some coherence. He has tried, keeping in mind the legal independence of the former agencies, to work in that direction. I doubt that anything of significance will come of this. Perhaps we should seriously consider a constitutional amendment to eliminate the independent regulatory agencies—to put them back into the executive branch where they really belong and thus force Congress to come to grips with the fundamental policy issues.

Whether one talks about the Federal Election Commission or the Environmental Protection Agency (already part of the executive branch) or the Federal Trade Commission or the Interstate Commerce Commission or the Civil Aeronautics Board, one is talking about agencies that have enormous policy-making roles. Is it right in a democracy that those policy-making roles should be immune—as they largely are today—from the political process? Should not some component of our political system (and only the president has power over the execution of policy) have the responsibility of trying to stitch together what are often palpably inconsistent policies?

Sears, Roebuck, Inc., in a dramatic, though in my opinion unsound, legal gesture, sued the government, asking, in effect, that a federal district judge coordinate the Equal Employment Opportunity activities of the American government. This becomes necessary largely because the EEOC is an independent regulatory agency, although it is related to the Labor Department and other agencies such as the Civil Service Commission. What we have really created is a mishmash. The federal judge, properly, in my judgment, declined that role. This supports my conclusion that the coordinator has to be the president. That is why I am seriously suggesting a constitutional amendment to eliminate the independent regulatory agencies. I would like to call that notion "Super Sunset."

The Record on Sunset Review of Two Agencies

Dennis Avery

The Commodity Futures Trading Commission (CFTC) last year became the first federal agency to go through a serious sunset review. Subsequently the Consumer Product Safety Commission (CPSC) went through a similar review. While I found very little to disagree with in the previous statements, I must say that on the basis of the CFTC and CPSC experiences, sunset legislation is unlikely to provide significant deregulatory benefits for the American people. Both the agencies that went through the experience went in weak but came out stronger, with stronger iron triangles and stronger budgetary positions.

The CFTC is a useful example. At the time it entered the reauthorization procedure, the commission had achieved a reputation throughout the government for poor management. It had spent half its three years' existence resolving an organization table for its 400 staff members. It had generated large amounts of opposition from the futures industry because of its significantly increased regulation of that industry. Perhaps more serious, the CFTC was accused of doing this not on the basis of need, but out of emulation of the Securities and Exchange Commission, where many of its lawyers received their early experience.

We had a Republican chairman, one of the few Republicans left in town. He was outspoken and active, but he freely admitted that he knew very little about the futures industry. We had made practically no effort as an agency to stay in close touch with our congressional oversight committees.

We had achieved public recognition mostly for negative achievements. For example, there had been a major default on the potato contract in New York. At the time we underwent reauthorization, it had been two years, but we had not completed any of our proceedings against the participants in that default. We were involved also in a noisy squabble with the Hunt oil family over soybean contracts in Chicago—and lost our first court action. Perhaps our biggest black eye, however, came from something called London commodity options. The commission had refused to permit organized exchanges in this country to trade these commodity options, but we had left a loophole permitting deal-

41

ers—who were not organized and were, incidentally, much more difficult to regulate—to do so. Unscrupulous people poured through that loophole, setting up boiler rooms throughout the country and bombarding the public at all hours of the day and night with long-distance phone calls touting these investments. Most of them were priced so high that buyers were unlikely ever to be able to exercise their options. When the buyer did have an exercisable option, the dealer in all too many cases had disappeared before the buyer could collect.

The commission had, at the time of review, been criticized by the securities administrators for discouraging them from assisting us in preventing the fraudulent operations of the London commodities options dealers and the sale of futures contracts in their states. We had also been criticized for leasing and outfitting plush quarters in downtown Washington.

The CFTC looked so weak that there developed a major competition to take away parts of our jurisdiction. The Chicago Board of Trade came forward and publicly announced its support for any legislation to return futures trading regulation to the Department of Agriculture. The SEC asked for jurisdiction over the new futures contracts in financial instruments, even though it had no jurisdiction over the instruments on which these contracts were based. The Treasury Department asked for jurisdiction over the Treasury bonds and Treasury bills that were being traded on futures, arguing that the futures contracts might complicate their debt management responsibility.

The General Accounting Office first said that our jurisdiction should be extended unchanged, then reversed itself to say that SEC and Treasury should have their requests granted. The Office of Management and Budget suggested that the CFTC be made part of the executive branch with a single administrator replacing the five-man commission. That suggestion came very late in the process; I do not believe it was seriously considered. It got so bad that someone wrote a letter putting forth the claim of the Bureau of Indian Affairs over our jurisdiction, pointing out that the BIA had interests in "certain hard commodities such as silver and turquoise in certain parts of Texas and Oklahoma" and noting also that the BIA for over a hundred years "has administered contracts for future delivery called Indian treaties, many of which were still open contracts today."

One major lesson clearly illustrated in the CFTC experience is that sunset is expensive. It costs a great deal of congressional time and a great deal of the agency's time. The General Accounting Office had a three-man team in CFTC for close to a year preparing for the sunset proceedings. The House Agricultural Appropriations Subcommittee had two men there for nine months. The House and Senate agriculture committees began their preparations with major inputs of staff time approximately six months before the proceedings started.

The proceedings themselves extended over several months, during which the commission members attended twenty-five separate hearings and formal meetings. The proceedings of the House Agriculture Committee alone ran to 765 printed pages. The results of the review appear to be negligible: the commission was extended for four more years with practically no change in its jurisdiction. The major change that came about was that our chairman no longer serves for a stated five-year term, but rather at the pleasure of the president. The commission also received a 10 percent increase in its budget and an 11 percent increase in its staff authorization.

These results are consistent with those of the CPSC hearings: that commission's jurisdiction was extended without change, the chairman resigned, and the $40 million budget cut that had been proposed for the agency was rescinded. In both these sunset reviews, the regulated industries shifted in midstream from opposition to support for the respective commissions.

Sunset seems to have achieved some success in dusty corners of state government, but can it work at the federal level? Both my commission and the CPSC believe—and with good reason—that the relationships with their industries and with their oversight committees have been greatly strengthened by this full review of what they were doing and why. The congressional committees in both cases now feel that their prestige is on the line with the agencies, and both sets of regulatees have decided they prefer the devils they know to the devils that they don't. In the case of the futures industry, there was stark terror at the possibility of having a triple set of regulators with split jurisdiction.

Another lesson that emerged is that it is difficult for Congress to evaluate an agency's performance. It is not easy for a congressional staff person, let alone a congressman, to master the technicalities involved. This will be a serious problem in relation to independent regulatory agencies because they deal with highly technical matters. It may be that if we have sunset, it will be useful only for addressing broad questions such as the validity of the agency's mission or making a general assessment of its cost-benefit ratio.

The third lesson is that sunset is expensive. A major sunset initiative would require either that the other activities of Congress come to a standstill or that the staffs be beefed up to cover this additional responsibility.

Finally and most important, the political forces that led to the creation of these agencies are going to be crucial factors working to maintain them. In the case of the CFTC, we faced a fast-growing market institution called futures trading, which appeared to be producing larger and larger economic benefits and which suffered major public distrust. Congress believed it had two choices in this review: it could either eliminate futures trading or continue to have some regulatory agency overseeing that activity.

I now offer five lessons learned from our review. First, we should not expect too much from sunset. If it could not terminate small agencies such as the CFTC and the CPSC, what could it terminate?

Second, sunset needs a long review period, and it is expensive. However, the questions have to be broad because there is no point in digging into technicalities. We should limit the review to such questions as, Is the agency needed? Does it have a favorable cost-benefit ratio? Have there been any changes in jurisdictional needs in the time since the last review?

Third, we can expect fierce interagency competition. There are very few activities in this government that cannot logically be placed in more than one agency. Sunset is a marvelous opportunity for bureaucratic ambush.

Fourth, we can expect that any agency with a sunset requirement will maintain extremely close liaison with its oversight committee—even showing slavish attention to the committee's wishes. This may be good; it may not. It depends on the committee and the agency.

Finally, any agency going through sunset will attempt to use the process to improve its position. I remind you that both the agencies that have gone through it so far have come out with stronger iron triangles and with larger budgets and staffs.

Summary of Discussion

In the discussion that followed the presentations on sunset review, a question from the floor raised the possibility of breaking up the iron triangle by forcing the costs of running an agency back on the regulated industry as a cost of being regulated. In response, Mr. Avery pointed out that the consumer will ultimately pay for the cost of regulating futures trading if the trading industry is asked to pay. That is true because those costs will be passed on in commodity prices just as the costs of the New York Stock Exchange are not absorbed by the securities industry but raise the cost to each investor of owning a security. Mr. Silberman suggested that the trucking industry would be delighted to pay the budget of the Interstate Commerce Commission, just as the airlines would the Civil Aeronautics Board. In his opinion the real objection to most regulation of a particular industry comes from a broader, consumer-oriented constituency.

Senator Percy viewed deregulation of the airline industry as easy compared with an anticipated "huge struggle" over deregulating rate setting in the trucking industry. In response to Mr. Silberman's question whether deregulation of trucking would include greater ease of entry into the industry, the senator pointed out that there is a strong coalition in favor of easing entry, in spite of present united opposition by teamsters and truckers.

The question arose whether some areas of legislation, such as the Voting Rights Act, ought to be exempt from sunset and, if so, what principles should be followed. Mr. Silberman replied that he had come to the conclusion that the extension (and the expansion) of the Voting Rights Act were "a bad mistake"—they had made it possible for the judiciary to get into areas far beyond any contemplated by the legislation. He felt that the act had "been a great success" and had "done its job" before extension and should have been allowed to expire.

The question of the costs of sunset review suggested by Mr. Avery was revived in the discussion. Senator Percy explained that there was not yet any real measure of sunset costs. He then discussed the costs imposed by regulation in general and focused on the indirect costs of

45

compliance, which the Ford administration had estimated at $100 billion. Mr. Silberman argued that the most important cost of regulation is the "diversion of creativity" within a regulated industry necessary to comply with regulation. Over time this appears to result in lessened activity and vigor on the part of management.

An expansion on Mr. Avery's contention that Congress would have no incentive at all to deregulate, given the existence and strength of iron triangles, produced a response from Mr. Silberman. In his opinion the lesson to draw from the experience of the Commodity Futures Trading Commission was that any review that focuses on only one activity of the federal government will be ineffective. A better strategy might be a comparison of different activities both to develop a clear understanding on the part of the general public of the trade-offs and conflicts involved and to force individual groups to compete against one another. This, in his opinion, should place more responsibility on the president, where the conflicts, trade-offs, and lost opportunity costs can be appreciated. It was suggested from the floor that Congress might be reluctant to shift responsibility to the president, but Mr. Silberman countered that because the proposed Government Accountability Act, which has passed the Senate once, requires the executive to rank programs within a department and over a period of time (regardless of which party is in the White House), there will be agreement on the least effective programs. These findings will generate great public attention because identifying winners and losers "absolutely commands attention in Washington." If this ranking requirement were extended to the independent regulatory agencies, such comparisons should also attract public attention. Unless you can mobilize the population at large, there is no chance for reform of the independent regulatory agencies, according to Mr. Silberman.

Senator Percy described his experience with the successful use of sunset review on a small scale to terminate presidential advisory committees and commissions (which totaled about 3,000). Over 800 have now been ended, saving millions of dollars. He explained that the Government Accountability Act would provide an "orderly means of sunsetting spending programs." Starting with an estimate of priorities from the Office of Management and Budget, the Congressional Budget Office would set its priorities, as would the comptroller general. Using an example of a public works tunnel project called TARP, Senator Percy stated that a comptroller general's report on its extraordinary cost overruns raised questions about its cost-effectiveness and led him to consider the project a candidate for sunset, even though it would aid fifty-four Illinois communities.

Part Three

The Legislative Veto

Introduction

Richard E. Cohen, Chairman

Using the legislative veto mechanism to reform federal regulation is a highly controversial proposal. Its two leading congressional advocates, Senator Schmitt and Congressman Levitas, report that it is gaining popularity on Capitol Hill. Antonin Scalia, a law professor who previously served as an assistant attorney general, presents a strong case for the opposition. The two sides disagree strongly about both the practical wisdom and the constitutionality of the device. It appears that the legislative veto will continue to create conflict between Congress and the executive branch until the Supreme Court intervenes and rules on the permissible extent of its use. So far, the court has avoided any direct consideration of the issue.

The political context for the legislative veto, Senator Schmitt points out, is the growing public frustration with the impact of federal regulations on economic growth and personal liberties. The growth in federal regulation has made "regulatory government a substitute for legislative government," in this view, and the "well-meaning bureaucrats" who draft these measures must be brought under closer control to avoid a further loss of public confidence in government. One way to control this development without excessive interference with necessary bureaucratic functions is to permit the Senate or House to disapprove a proposed regulation before it becomes effective.

Mr. Scalia counters that a lengthy series of studies has concluded that the legislative veto is unconstitutional because it ignores the role of the president in the making of laws. Congress cannot, in this view, "render a statute repealable" without the president's approval. In addition, the legislative veto ignores the principle of separation of powers, which gives the president the power to execute the laws and the judiciary the power to interpret them. The proposal merges powers that should be kept separate and as such is "fundamentally antidemocratic." Mr. Scalia sees the legislative veto and regulatory reform debates as a "sideshow" designed to give "the impression of prompt and vigorous congressional action" without really addressing the problems of excessive government regulation.

On the other hand, the courts have not found the legislative veto unconstitutional in cases where they could have done so, as Congressman Levitas points out. Pending such a decision, he believes the elected representatives of the public, not the "unelected bureaucracy," should have the power to make the laws in the United States. From this perspective, the legislative veto is "a recapturing for the people of their essential rights to have a major role in the lawmaking process."

There is no simple resolution of these disagreements. The legislative veto has already emerged as a major issue in the debate over extension of the Federal Trade Commission, and it is likely, because of its growing popularity on Capitol Hill, to be the cause of significant contention between Congress and the executive during the 96th Congress.

Putting Democratic Controls on the Law of Bureaucrats

Harrison H. Schmitt

One of the most disturbing lessons I have learned as a senator is that a new category of law, regulatory law, is imposing itself more and more on the average law-abiding American. The dominant legal force in our society has become the law of the bureaucrat, rather than the law created by elected representatives in Congress.

Federal regulations are frustrating the economic growth and personal will of our citizens. They are alienating people from their government. Unless the well-meaning bureaucrats who create these rules are brought under the control of the public, through their elected representatives, our people will continue to suffer from a crisis of confidence and lack of faith in our government.

The peril we face is real and tangible. New regulatory law required 60,000 pages in the 1978 *Federal Register*. The cost of federal regulations to the private sector alone will be over $100 billion in 1979. The annual rate of increase of this cost is over 15 percent.

By a ratio of 18 to 1, regulatory law outnumbers the statutes passed by Congress. This regulatory law is created by nonelected public officials—the bureaucrats who, even with the best of intentions, cannot speak for the people. In this making of modern law, the public has had little or no impact. So-called public hearings are commonly held at inconvenient times and places, and they often appear, to my constituents at least, to have little or no impact on the nature of the final rule.

Likewise, our elected representatives have had little or no input into the "promulgation" of regulations beyond passing some vague policy statute that authorizes some unknown "secretary" or unknown "administrator" to "promulgate such rules and regulations as necessary to carry out the provisions of the Act." Thus, the Congress turns its back on both the public and the bureaucrats. The public then bears the burden of unnecessary, extravagant, or unintended regulations, and the conscientious bureaucrat bears the brunt of public criticism. The sword cuts two ways.

The last few decades have seen a rapid increase in regulatory government as a substitute for legislative government. As the bureaucracy has mushroomed, everyone has acquired a personal horror story to tell about the loss of his or her freedom to the government. Unexplained termination of retirement or disability benefits, delay in construction, the cost and frustration of unnecessary and unused paperwork, the unheard-of tax rule, the loss of a livelihood, and the unfeeling attitude of an impersonal government have an all-too-familiar ring to each of us in Congress. The government we all want to believe, the government we all want to respect, the government we all want to help those who cannot help themselves, the government of the people, by the people, and for the people has become a government of derision, of bad jokes and roadblocks to the well-being of its citizens.

Against this backdrop, there is an innovative concept of government that is getting a great deal of attention in this Congress, in the last Congress, and increasingly through the last few years. It is called the legislative veto.

I personally am a newcomer to this—I am a newcomer to Congress. I must acknowledge at this point the leadership of Congressman Elliott Levitas in the House through the years before my arrival on the scene. Unfortunately the Senate did not pay much attention to the legislative veto until the last Congress, when we were able to get hearings begun to examine that concept.

The legislative veto is conceived by us as a means for elected representatives to exert tangible control over the making of regulatory law while at the same time avoiding excessive interference with the necessary administrative functions of the bureaucracy. The most attractive version of the legislative veto is a procedure that would allow either the Senate or the House to vote to disapprove a proposed regulation during a sixty-day period following the publication of a final rule. If one house voted to veto the proposed rule, the other house would have thirty days to override or "veto" that action, thus allowing the proposed rule to become law.

The bill I and twenty cosponsors have introduced in the 96th Congress to implement this procedure is numbered S. 104 and entitled the Regulatory Reduction and Congressional Control Act. Its sister bill in the House is H.R. 1776. The Senate bill, unlike the House bill, as I understand it, would require that an economic impact analysis of the proposed rule be submitted first to the public and finally to Congress for evaluation during the consideration period. The bill also stipulates that agencies must reconsider and repromulgate an existing regulation if one house so votes. This provision would allow for careful public and congressional review of controversial regulations that are already on the books and to some considerable degree offers an alternative to sunset legislation.

It is important to point out that the legislative veto contained in S. 104 would not require Congress to review any or all rules promulgated by a department or agency. That would be both impractical and undesirable. The bill simply provides an improved opportunity for congressional review and, when it is deemed necessary by a majority of one house of Congress, disapproval of a proposed or existing rule.

The legislative process set down by the framers of the Constitution is remarkable in its pragmatism and common sense. However, the Founding Fathers could never have foreseen our present danger—the danger of the all-consuming bureaucracy our times have forced upon us. The legislative veto is a means to return legislative responsibility to elected representatives while at the same time improving the quality of necessary administrative action. I believe this procedure is an important addition to the structure of representative democracy.

Several objections have been raised with regard to providing Congress with this tool. The most frequent is the claim that the one-house legislative veto may be unconstitutional. Although the general constitutional question relating to the legislative veto has not been definitively ruled upon by the Supreme Court, on the several occasions where the legislative veto has been challenged in the courts, it has not been ruled unconstitutional. Since 1932 Congess has enacted over 295 provisions of law with legislative review or veto powers.

In *Atkins* v. *United States*, 140 federal judges challenged the constitutionality of the congressional veto provision contained in the Federal Salary Act. In its decision, the court of claims concluded that the legislative veto represented "a device authorized by Article I, Section 1 of the Constitution, coupled with the necessary and proper clause, and that it contravenes neither the broad principle of the separation of powers nor any specific provision of the Constitution." The Supreme Court refused to review this court of claims action, thereby lending finality to the decision.

In *Buckley* v. *Valeo*, the Supreme Court did not decide the case on the basis of the legislative veto, but Justice Byron White expressed his opinion in dicta that it is constitutional. He stated, "I am also of the view that the otherwise valid power of a properly created independent agency is not rendered constitutionally infirm, as violative of the President's veto power, by a statutory provision subjecting agency regulations to disapproval by either House of Congress."

The legislative veto, in the form of a simple resolution of disapproval, is the sole means whereby Congress can quickly and with precision overturn a rule and return it to the promulgating body for reconsideration. This procedure does not require Congress to pass judgment on every rule. In fact, experience with nearly 300 statutes containing legislative review or disapproval procedures demonstrates that the tool is rarely used, but it is extraordinarily influential in affecting administrative action. Just recently, for example, the question of gas rationing was dealt with under a legislative veto provision.

Many state governments have successfully experimented with this concept, as well as with other forms of legislative review of agency rule making. State legislatures with veto authority over regulations have seldom found it necessary to exercise that authority. Its primary value is as a deterrent to ensure that agencies will not stray beyond the bounds of legislative intent when promulgating rules. These states have found that just the existence of the review process has vastly improved the performance of the affected agencies.

The legislative veto contained in S. 104 will ensure that federal regulations are a mirror of legislative intent and do not abuse economic common sense. It will demonstrate to the people of our country that Congress is willing to reassume its responsibility as the lawmaking branch of the federal government. The time is long overdue for the elected representatives of the people to act to return to Congress its constitutional responsibility for the quantity and quality of law governing the American people.

We must place some limitation on those actions of a legislative character that, through delegation, Congress has come close to surrendering to a growing, unelected, bureaucratic fourth branch of government. It is my opinion that the legislative veto fulfills a critical need at this crossroads in our nation's history.

The Legislative Veto:
In Violation of the Constitution

Antonin Scalia

I want to speak about the constitutional aspects of the legislative veto and then about some of the practicalities. But first, to clear away some of the underbrush: The judges' case mentioned by Senator Schmitt—if you think the court of claims a very persuasive authority for this constitutional law issue—involved a situation in which the plaintiff judges wanted to eat their cake and have it too. That is, they were challenging a statute that permitted judicial salaries to be raised by the president subject to a legislative veto. They were urging the court to keep part of this statute and throw away the rest—to keep the raise and throw away the veto. The Department of Justice did not even argue the legislative veto issue in its brief, because it maintained that the issue did not have to be reached. Whether the veto was valid or invalid, the judges lose. If it was valid, their pay raise had properly been vetoed. If it was invalid, the whole scheme—not only the veto but also the pay raise to which it was attached—would fall. I believe that the government's position on this point was correct and that the court's exposition on the legislative veto was unnecessary to the outcome. In any event, only four of the seven judges thought the legislative veto constitutional. And they did this, as I have said, without benefit of a government brief on the point.

The legislative veto is in fact a very new device. It does not appear on the statute books for the first century and a half of our nation's history. This immediately makes one wonder: if it is such a potent device, if it gives Congress so much power, why would Congress not have used it for 150 years? The answer quite simply is that it is unconstitutional.

I am quite serious. A consistent abstention over that long a period of time from the founding of the Constitution, with respect to a device that is as much in the interest of Congress as this one, is very persuasive that Congress thought there was something wrong with it. And indeed Congress did. There is an 1898 study by the Senate Judiciary Committee whose conclusion suggests the unconstitutionality of the legislative veto. Leaders of Congress have asserted its unconstitutionality, as have

55

all presidents since it first appeared. The Justice Department has consistently opposed it in all its manifestations—although the present attorney general maintains its constitutionality in the one area of executive reorganization (a distinction I cannot understand).

The principal constitutional arguments that have been made against the legislative veto are twofold. The first is based on Article I, Section 7, of the Constitution, which provides for the president's participation in the legislative process. That section states, first, that no bill can become law until it is presented to the president for his approval. If he approves it, it becomes law; if he disapproves, it must be repassed by the Congress by two-thirds vote.

If that were the only provision of Article I, Section 7, there would be some argument about whether the legislative veto is good, bad, or indifferent. But the records of the debate at the constitutional convention show that the Founding Fathers were troubled about saying that only *bills* require presidential approval. They were concerned about Congress's passing "resolutions" or "directives" or "senses of Congress" that would not be presented to the president for approval because he was only entitled to approve bills. They decided that another clause was needed to prevent the Congress from making law without calling it law. So Article I, Section 7, contains, in addition to the bill veto provision, an entirely separate veto provision that applies to "every order, resolution, or vote to which the concurrence of the Senate and House of Representatives may be necessary." Such action must be presented to the president for his approval, just like a bill.

There is here a side issue, which I do not want to get into very deeply. The provision does apply only when concurrence of *both* houses is necessary. It could be argued that a one-house veto does not meet this description—so that a one-house veto is constitutional although a two-house veto is not. Such a result would of course be absurd. The explanation of the absurdity is that even when a legislative veto provision permits action by a single house, the concurrence of the other house is still "necessary" under the Constitution itself, the very first section of which decrees that "all legislative powers . . . shall be vested in a Congress of the United States, which shall consist of a Senate and a House of Representatives." In other words, in addition to violating the veto clause, the one-house veto violates a totally separate principle of the Constitution—the bicamerality of the legislative branch.

It seems to me the intent of the Constitution is clear. Congress is not supposed to take any action having the force and effect of law without going through the presidential veto process. Thus, the question comes down to whether a legislative veto has the force and effect of law. Surely no one would contend that if a statute (without a legislative veto provision) authorizes an agency to issue regulations, those regulations can be set aside by the vote of one house or even of both houses. Such action by Congress would in effect be amending the law: the agency had the power to issue regulations; now Congress is saying it does not have the power. Quite clearly, such a change in the law would have to be made by statute. The proponents of the legislative veto say this situation is changed when the original statute that confers the power to issue regulations specifies that those regulations must be presented to Congress for its veto. But I see no way in which the mere recitation of an unconstitutional arrangement in the original legislation can validate that arrangement. Can Congress, for instance, render a statute repealable without presidential participation simply by saying in the statute, "This law shall continue in effect unless and until Congress, without presidential approval, declares it terminated"? Surely not. And I see no reason why a similar recitation with respect to the revision of agency authority is any different.

The supporters of the legislative veto would found a distinction upon the notion that, when agency action is subjected to a veto in the enabling statute, the agency never *had* unrestricted power to take the action—and thus the veto does not alter agency power and does not "change" the law. But of course the same could be said of the repealable statute I just mentioned: it never *had* open-ended existence but was always subject to congressional destruction, and thus the law is not "changed" when the repealer is exercised. It seems to me the proponents of the legislative veto are caught on the horns of a dilemma. An enabling statute that contains a veto provision either confers on the agency power to take certain action or does not. If it does, the exercise of the veto restricts that power and constitutes a change in the law. If it does not, the original "law" is really meaningless and constitutes merely an announcement of congressional intent to determine the scope of agency power at a later date—in which case it is that *later* determination (to veto or not to veto) that is the real legislative decision in which the president must participate. (I happen to think this is the more realistic way of looking at the situation; and it would require presidential participation even in the decision *not* to veto—a requirement that may be satisfied when vetoable regulations are proposed by executive branch agencies but not when they are proposed by independent regulatory agencies over which the president has no control.) Either way, a legislative veto through a process other than that provided by Article I, Section 7, violates the Constitution.

The second constitutional principle that is violated is not stated as explicitly in the Constitution as the veto provision but is even more fundamental. That is the principle of separation of powers, reflected in the division of the first three articles, the first saying that all legislative power resides in a Congress, the second that the executive power is vested in a president of the United States, and the third that the judicial power is vested in the Supreme Court and such inferior courts as Congress may establish. You are all familiar with the separation of powers. The theory is that, once a law is passed, its execution belongs to the executive, not to Congress, and its interpretation to the judiciary. This separation of powers is considered a major barrier against despotism, as you will recollect from Montesquieu and the *Federalist* papers.

Once Congress passes a law, its job is done except for overseeing the way the law is being applied and interpreted—and, if it is dissatisfied with that, passing such amendments as may be necessary. The legislative veto changes all that. Congress in effect says, without enacting any new legislation, that this application of the law in regulations is okay, that application of the law in regulations is not. It is a fundamental merging of powers that are supposed to be separate.

To reduce the matter to the absurd, suppose Congress enacts a statute that says the president can do whatever he wants, provided that he clears it with Congress, through a legislative veto process, before doing it. What is the effect of that law? It is to render every executive action reviewable by Congress. Congress would be the ultimate referee of all executive functions. Now that is reducing the matter to the absurd, but the legislative veto applies the same principle on a more limited basis.

To these constitutional arguments, the following reply is sometimes made: "Let us be realistic. What you say may be theoretically true, but in practice there is no real alteration in the balance of power between the president and Congress because the president would not even have this power unless there were a veto attached to it. For example, Congress would not have given the president the power to establish judicial and congressional salaries unless it had the legislative veto attached. Realistically, then, the president has lost nothing."

That argument, in many cases, seems true enough. But it disregards a third constitutional objection to the legislative veto, one not often made because it does not pertain to executive prerogatives (and most of the attacks on the legislative veto have come from the executive branch). That objection is this: The separation of powers is not meant merely to protect the executive branch from the legislature; it is also— and more fundamentally—meant to protect the people from a combination of the executive and the legislature; and when the principle is violated, it is the people who are hurt, not just the president.

The legislative veto upsets the constitutional scheme by permitting laws to be passed without going through the troublesome process of legislation. What the Founding Fathers thought about the process of legislation can be seen in the *Federalist* papers. Here Madison is talking about the advantage of having a Senate:

> Another advantage accruing from the ingredients of equal State representation in the Senate is the additional impediment that must prove against improper acts of legislation. No law or resolution can now be passed without the concurrence first of a majority of the people and then of a majority of the States. It must be acknowledged that this complicated check on legislation in some instances can be injurious as well as beneficial, but as the facility and excess of lawmaking seem to be the diseases to which our governments are most liable [nothing has changed] it is not impossible that this part of the Constitution may be more convenient in practice than it appears to many in contemplation.

Yes, the process of legislation is a pain in the neck. There are interest groups here, interest groups there; one person wants this, another that; and the member of Congress must stand up on the floor and vote yes or no. He is bound to lose support on one side or the other. It is all terribly inconvenient, and it certainly slows down the process of legislation. How much easier it is to arrange things so that the law can be changed without any congressional vote! And this is precisely what the legislative veto achieves.

You may recall the 30 percent congressional pay increase that went through in 1977. It was proposed by President Ford after the 1976 election, and it became law. Because Congress stood up and voted for it? No, because Congress declined to veto it. There was no one to point a finger at except a president who had already lost his bid for reelection. The legislative veto is fundamentally antidemocratic, which is precisely why it has been used in such matters as congressional pay raises and executive branch reorganization. It permits change of the law (by which I mean final congressional decision on a matter on which Congress has previously—through adoption of a legislative veto clause—reserved judgment) without the inconvenience and the protection of the democratic process.

Let me discuss briefly now the practicalities of the legislative veto. The only serious study of its actual operation—conducted by Professors Bruff and Gellhorn and published in the *Harvard Law Review*—found that virtually none of the promised advantages in fact ensue. The Office of Education of the Department of Health, Education and Welfare has been subject to a legislative veto over all its rule making since 1974. Is it more "under control" than other portions of the federal bureaucracy? Hardly.

Why have all the promised wonders not come to pass? Except for avoidance of the presidential veto and of the democratic controls over the legislative process (the requirement that Congress vote yes or no), nothing can be accomplished by the legislative veto that cannot be accomplished equally well by the following simple steps: one, a thirty-day waiting period for all regulations; two, a modification of the internal rules and procedures of the Senate and the House to provide that any committee proposal to overturn a proposed regulation shall come immediately to the floor and be voted on. That will achieve everything that the legislative veto now achieves, except that (1) it will not avoid the president's veto and (2) it will not avoid the necessity of Congress's standing up to be counted with respect to those issues it has not yet resolved, instead of resolving them through silent acceptance of the agency resolution.

Far from controlling bureaucracy, there is a good chance that the legislative veto will multiply bureaucracy. One of the conclusions of the Bruff/Gellhorn study is the following: "Most of the effective review occurred at the committee or subcommittee level, often focusing on the concerns of a single chairman or member. Indeed"—this is the crucial point—"much settlement of policy occurred in behind-the-scenes negotiations between the staffs of the committees and the agencies." So instead of one bureaucracy, you have two: one that writes the regulation and one that reviews it. The two sit down, trade back and forth, sometimes play off their principals against one another: "We would like to change this provision, Senator, but the agency is really adamant about it." (The executive bureaucrats, in discussions with their politically appointed superiors, attribute the same adamancy to Congress.) I have seen that process work, and it is lovely.

Finally, even if, as I doubt, the legislative veto is entirely harmless, its main vice is the vice of all ineffectual remedies. It gives the patient the false sense that he is being treated for what ails him and thus deters him from seeking a genuine cure. The legislative veto and, I might add, many of the so-called regulatory reform initiatives that tinker with agency and congressional procedures are a sideshow. They are designed to give the impression of prompt and vigorous congressional action, but they do not address the real problem at all. The real problem is not congressional power to reverse the agencies. Congress has that power and has always had it. The question is congressional will or congressional capacity.

If Congress were to be frank with the American people, it would say to them:

Fellow citizens, your federal government is simply doing too much for you to expect *us* to exercise substantial control over it. We have, to be sure, the *power* to control; we can pass laws. But we have no more hours in the day than the first Congress had and an almost unimaginable number of existing programs to keep track of, not to mention a steady stream of new legislative proposals. We have handled the problem in the only way possible—by enacting vague and general laws that confer substantial powers on the agencies, since we have neither the time nor the knowledge to get into too many specifics ourselves.

You now seem to be chafing at a perceived loss of popular control over your government. But you must face the fact that no single level of genuinely democratic government can solve all your real problems or right all your real wrongs—not even all those that lend themselves to governmental solution. If you want the broad scope of beneficial federal action to which you have become accustomed (we presume you consider it beneficial, since you keep reelecting us), like it or not, many basic policy judgments are going to have to be left to bureaucracies, either an exclusively executive bureaucracy or a combined executive-congressional bureaucracy.

That is the road we have chosen, fellow citizens. Learn to love it—or else tell us where you want to constrict the expansion of federal regulation and services. But you cannot sensibly tell us to "get control" of the agencies and at the same time demand an increase in their number and functions. It cannot be done.

That, I suggest, would be an honest description of the real regulatory crisis we are facing and would place the real choice clearly before the American people. To cover it over with cheap paint, such as the legislative veto and much other "procedural reform," is to be worse than merely ineffective. It is to consign genuine democratic government to a slow death, the beginnings of which we sense about us.

The Veto as an Exercise of Congressional Responsibility

Elliott H. Levitas

I would like to deal with the political aspects of the legislative veto as they will develop during the 96th Congress and beyond. The constitutionality issue is intriguing because, despite everything Professor Scalia has said, no court that has dealt with the matter of legislative veto has found it unconstitutional. As I have said on other occasions to Attorney General Griffin Bell, to Professor Scalia, to President Carter, and to members of the House, the ultimate decision about constitutionality will not be made by any of us. It will eventually be made by a court. In the meantime, no amount of argument by attorneys general or even the higher authority of law professors will resolve the constitutional issue.

Therefore, instead of dealing with the points that Professor Scalia has raised, I will move on to the political issues involved. When Professor Scalia says that it is fundamentally undemocratic or antidemocratic to let elected officials make ultimate decisions on legislative matters, it makes me feel that we are seeing the subject through a looking glass—seeing the reverse of the truth. There is nothing more fundamental to our whole system of government than that people elected by the citizens of this country should and must have the ultimate responsibility for legislation.

Regulations issued by administrative agencies, both executive agencies and, even more significantly, independent agencies, have the force of law. People can go to jail, they can lose property, they can be fined, they can lose benefits and entitlements—all on the basis of regulations issued by people unaccountable to the public and even unknown to most. Regulations are law in every sense of the word. They are not merely the execution of the law—arresting someone for violating a law—they are laws in and of themselves. The issue, therefore, is very simple, regardless of how we may decorate it and regardless of the nuances of whether we have a one-house veto, a two-house veto, or the modified one-house veto that Senator Schmitt and I advocate in S. 104 and H.R. 1776. Whichever approach one takes, the question at issue boils down to this: Who makes the laws in the United States? Is it the unelected bureaucracy, or should it be the elected representatives of the people in Congress?

Senator Schmitt and I say that laws should be made by the elected representatives, through whom the people make their will felt. We advocate the legislative veto as a recapturing for the people of their essential right to have a major role in the lawmaking process.

When the legislative veto has begun to surface as a major issue, and it will, I predict what may be the most dramatic confrontation between the executive and legislative branches during the 96th Congress. When this issue first arose, very few people paid attention to it. As word got about to the nation and to Congress, however, the legislative veto became more and more popular and more and more demanding of a decision. S. 104 presently has 24 cosponsors in the Senate, and H.R. 1776, at last count, 180 cosponsors in the House. I suspect it will have well over 200 by Independence Day.

During the last Congress, the legislative veto issue was raised primarily by the House of Representatives through amendments to several pieces of legislation. Perhaps the best known involved the Federal Trade Commission authorization legislation, to which the House attached a legislative veto of the commission's regulations. When the bill went to conference with the Senate, which had included no legislative veto, the Conference Committee dropped the provision. The Senate adopted the conference report, but the House, by an almost two to one vote, rejected it. The matter went back to conference later in 1978, and this time some kind of Mickey Mouse legislative review procedure was written in. When it came back to the House, a substantial majority again rejected the authorization of the FTC for 1979.

This action was unprecedented; no one can recall in recent history a reauthorization bill defeated in a conference report. This illustrates the tremendous sentiment for this concept in the House, a sentiment that I believe is growing in the Senate. The issue will come up again in the 96th Congress, quite early in the case of the FTC authorization. The House Commerce Committee has already reported out the FTC's reauthorization and, having learned well the lesson of the last Congress, has written the legislative veto into the bill that will come to the floor of the House. I predict it will be adopted overwhelmingly.

I predict that if the bill does not contain a legislative veto when it comes back from conference, the FTC authorization will again be defeated. Other pieces of legislation coming through the House and the Senate will bear legislative veto provisions on a serial basis, where appropriate, and I predict that support for them will grow in both houses of Congress.

There is already a growing realization of the importance of the legislative veto in the Senate, under the leadership of Senator Schmitt with the cooperation of Senator Nunn, Senator Levin, and others. More and more senators are realizing that they, too, run for reelection and that they, too, have to be accountable to the electorate. Many of the new members of the Senate came from the House, and all but one of these were cosponsors of legislative veto legislation in the House. For these reasons, I predict that sentiment will change dramatically in the coming months in the Senate.

In the House of Representatives, the major comprehensive legislation that applies to all agencies is H.R. 1776. In the past, the Rules Committee has often been a major stumbling block, responding primarily to pressures from the leadership who were, in turn, acting under pressures from certain interest groups and from the White House. The current Rules Committee, however, recognizes that it can no longer simply block a provision that has such strong support in the House and has established a special task force. Under the leadership of Congressman John Moakley, the task force has recently started its work. It is a commitment to me and to the members of the House that the Rules Committee will go forward in good faith with consideration of the legislative veto. I predict that comprehensive legislation on this subject will come to a vote in the House of Representatives early in the second session of the 96th Congress, after the task force has completed its work.

I am even seeing some reaction in the administration itself. No administration is likely to react favorably to a legislative veto, but I see signs that the executive branch recognizes the inevitability of some such provision and may be moving toward some type of accommodation.

On the other hand, there is some resistance to the legislative veto in Congress. Although the resistance does not represent anything close to a majority, it still exists because many members of the House and the Senate do not want to deal with the decisions it would present to them. It is much easier to pass legislation about cleaning up the air, purifying our waters, creating healthy and safe working environments, ending discrimination—these are all popular issues that members of Congress love to vote for and brag about when they are back home.

What we do not like to do, when those broad policies are translated into regulations, is to acknowledge that that is where lawmaking has really occurred. During a recent debate on this issue in the House, a distinguished and well-known colleague of mine argued against the legislative veto: "Do you understand what it would mean if we passed the Levitas amendment for legislative veto? Why, it means we have got to assume the responsibility for the regulations." That was a very candid statement, and a precisely accurate one as well.

Today, Congress chastises the bureaucracy with the same fervor as the American public does, but it also says we are not responsible for what they do. A legislative veto would not only place the responsibility where it lies, in the elected and accountable officials of the Congress, but it would also make Congress a great deal more sensitive about the delegation of that power to begin with, with appropriate guidelines, with appropriate standards. As a result, when we have to deal with the legislative veto of regulations, we would be dealing with something that we know is a better work product than is being turned out today. Therefore, we would get better laws and better and more responsive regulations. Most important, we will have answered the question, Who makes the laws in the United States? Is it the unelected bureaucracy or the elected officials in Congress? That answer will be the elected Congress.

Summary of Discussion

In the discussion that followed the presentations on the legislative veto, a questioner raised the possibility of placing all the regulatory agencies under the control of the president. Senator Schmitt said there already are too many departments for the president to administer. Mr. Scalia, however, said the idea makes sense because of the need for better coordination of government actions. Congressman Levitas saw the growing conflict among agencies as another argument for the legislative veto because of the need for accountability to the public.

Mr. Scalia used the discussion of President Carter's gasoline rationing plan to argue that the legislative veto is a "buck-passing mechanism." Senator Schmitt disagreed, saying that problems with the bill resulted from political mishandling by the White House. Yet Mr. Scalia maintained that the basic difficulty is that Congress has tried to regulate more than it can keep track of, and it has neither the time nor the inclination in many cases to explain what it means. Senator Schmitt again answered that the legislative veto permits the "diligent, conscientious" Senate or House member to see that the laws are reviewed by Congress.

Part Four

The Regulatory Budget

Introduction

Marvin H. Kosters, Chairman

Regulation has emerged as the federal government's predominant response to health, safety, environmental, and other concerns. Most of the goals of the regulations are worthwhile and widely shared, but increased recognition of the pervasiveness of regulation and of the magnitude of the compliance costs it entails has raised questions about the process. The questions concern not only who is "minding the store" but also whether our institutions and procedures are adequate to the task. How are decisions made about the amount of resources that should be devoted to improved health or safety in a particular industry or improved environmental purity in a particular area? What kind of information is available to make judgments on such questions? Is there a systematic framework for making these assessments?

The regulatory budget concept has been proposed as a way of providing a systematic framework for analysis and a tool to assist in establishing priorities. The concept as well as the name is analogous to the familiar fiscal budget—its role in the analysis and weighing of alternatives would be similar. Devoting resources to the pursuit of regulatory goals means that those resources are not available for other uses, just as when resources are devoted under the fiscal budget to such goals as highways or national defense. A regulatory budget would require estimates of the resource costs incurred in carrying out and complying with regulation. While the costs to government of carrying out regulation are included in the fiscal budget, the costs to private firms and individuals and to other institutions of meeting regulatory requirements have not been estimated in a comprehensive and systematic way so that they can be weighed against competing objectives of society.

One aspect of developing a regulatory budget process would be to establish a comprehensive and consistent framework for assembling the resource costs attributable to government regulation. Procedures and conventions would be needed for developing estimates of the costs of compliance because such estimates do not arise, even in retrospect, from the government's normal administrative and accounting procedures. This presents obvious—but not insurmountable—difficulties, although we would undoubtedly have to accept margins of error similar to those of fiscal budget estimates.

The other major aspect of the regulatory budget approach is the set of procedures to be used for proposing, reviewing, and approving the pattern of resources allocated to meeting regulatory goals. In this context the regulatory budget would provide a framework for systematically weighing and balancing objectives. It would involve assignment of priorities in deciding both the total resources to be devoted to meeting the goals of regulation and how those resources should be divided among competing regulatory objectives. An overall regulatory budget would bring to the surface for broader political consideration choices that are currently being made implicitly as the outcome of activities of numerous, narrowly focused agencies.

Congressman Brown, who has introduced legislation to establish a regulatory budget, sees the proposal as contributing to more informed regulatory decision making and thus to the furtherance of regulatory goals. Mr. Nader, on the other hand, sees the problem as insufficient and inadequate regulation, not as a need for containment. He stresses the merit of current regulatory procedures in ensuring access to proponents of regulatory initiatives and other affected parties, and notes also the difficulty of making cost estimates. A particular concern is that costs might receive too much weight as against human health and lives. Mr. Kristol believes we need to focus on achieving "reasonable aims through reasonable means." In his view the current regulatory process is not conducive to reasonable regulation because the costs it can impose are not subject to limits. In the absence of mechanisms for balancing objectives, movements are inclined to pursue limited objectives too far since they need not assume responsibility for broader consequences.

Legislating a Regulatory Budget Limit

Clarence J. Brown

Public reaction to burdensome federal regulation may be to this Congress what taxes, government spending, and Proposition 13 were to the 95th Congress—a force demanding a change in government policy.

Ralph Nader and his colleagues have performed a significant public service in protecting the health and safety of our society, in securing a cleaner environment. I applaud them for what they have done. I would not turn back the clock simply because regulatory policies have entailed some social costs; they have also produced substantial benefits for the public.

It is time, however, to take a hard look at the cost side of the problem, which has thus far been neglected. There are many situations in which the cost burdens far exceed the benefits to society, and those impacts clearly deserve attention.

I have been amazed at the recent flap over the proposed regulations declaring drilling muds, oil production brines, and crude oil residue "hazardous wastes." The Environmental Protection Agency recently proposed regulations that the American Petroleum Institute says will cost over $45 billion to implement. That is an interesting figure. It is twice as much as the industry's 1979 budget for drilling, exploration, and production of gas and oil. It is somewhere between $4 billion and $6 billion more than our OPEC oil import bill in 1978.

Even these huge costs might be worth it if the regulations were necessary, but they seem, on examination, not to be. The plain fact is that we have lived with these wastes for decades now with no apparent harm that anyone can identify. They simply are not hazardous. Enough has already been done to drive up energy costs and discourage domestic production and exploration without having EPA add its $45 billion worth.

The *Wall Street Journal* noted in a May 9 editorial: "Maybe EPA's extravagance will provoke Congress to legislate a regulatory budget limiting the cost agencies can impose on the economy. If so, the new regs proposed by EPA will have served a good purpose." I agree with this. Obviously, I understand that there are legislative efforts under way to block the proposed regulations by exempting muds and brines from coverage under the Resource Conservation and Recovery Act, pending a study to be completed within two years. Still, the proposal in itself will cost money, regardless of whether the regulations ever go into effect.

We do indeed need a regulatory budget to bring a little sanity and vision to the process. Our regulations run the gamut from sewage treatment plants to scrubbers on smokestacks, to beepers to warn workers when a truck is backing up, to earmuffs to protect workers from noise—including, presumably, the noise from the beepers on trucks—to flashing lights that we put on the trucks that are backing up. Many of our regulations are contradictory and superfluous. Raymond Hasty, president of the Park Sausage Company, made the point when he stated recently before the Joint Economic Committee: "USDA requires that our sausage kitchen floor be washed repeatedly for sanitary reasons. Yet OSHA rules floors must be dry. What's a man to do?"

Over the past decade we have witnessed a huge explosion of these regulations. Currently, the *Code of Federal Regulations* totals 800,000 pages and occupies fifty-two large bookshelves. Twenty years ago the whole thing was about ankle-high on me, but now I cannot reach to the top of that shelf of books stacked end to end, and I am six foot four.

Murray Weidenbaum, in a study for the Joint Economic Committee, recently reported that the 1979 costs of regulation were $102.7 billion, $97.9 billion in the private sector for compliance and $4.8 billion in agency administrative costs. Those are only the direct dollar costs, not the indirect or secondary costs, of regulation. Regulation discourages capital investment by introducing uncertainties in the investment decision process. I met with a group of people from the oil and gas industry this morning. They said: "We would just like to get Congress to do something—regulate, deregulate, put on a tax—but let us know as soon as you can what it is so we can go out and make our plans. We have to wait for your decision before we can make ours." Regulations cause losses in productivity, too, losses that the Brookings Institution estimates at about one-fourth of the potential increase in our society. Regulation also aggravates inflation by putting upward pressure on prices throughout the economy.

To help bring some sanity to the situation, I introduced in the House of Representatives, and Senator Lloyd Bentsen introduced in the Senate, a package of four bills to ease the regulatory burden. Our bills would do the following things:

● H.R. 75 provides that federal agencies, when they promulgate regulations, must select the most cost-effective method of meeting regulatory compliance.

- H.R. 76, the Regulatory Budget Act, provides for a procedure under which Congress would annually set a limit on the amount of private-sector compliance costs each federal agency can require by its regulations.

- H.R. 77, the Independent Agency Regulatory Improvement Act, extends the provisions of an executive order issued by President Carter that called for economic impact analyses to seventeen independent agencies not covered by the original executive order.

- H.R. 78, the Regulatory Conflicts Elimination Act, provides for a procedure under which conflicting and duplicative federal regulations would be eliminated.

It is the Regulatory Budget Act that is at issue here.

Current regulatory procedures fail to recognize that the goals of regulatory programs must be balanced against other national objectives, in much the same way that the goals of the federal government must be balanced and are balanced, for good or ill, through the federal budget process of direct spending. The achievement of any objective, public or private, demands resources that could be used for other purposes. Even if *all* regulations were cost-effective, we would still need to establish priorities for use of our limited resources.

In the past the fiscal budget was adequate for showing the impact of the federal government on the domestic economy because almost all federal government activities were direct—direct taxation and direct spending. If we added the financial commitments that are not direct, such as subsidized loans, loan guarantees, perhaps insurance programs—the so-called off-budget items—we got an even clearer picture of what the federal government was doing in the economy. However, with the recent rapid growth of new regulatory agencies—the Occupational Safety and Health Administration, the Environmental Protection Agency, the National Highway Traffic Safety Administration, and many others—the federal budget no longer conveys a complete picture of government impact and certainly does not convey the cost of government to our society. Since government has required the private sector to spend, for instance, for automobile safety, that clearly adds to the cost of the product. Mine safety, pollution control, and consumer protection all require private-sector expenditures that are not reflected in the federal budget.

Of course, there are also the paperwork costs, which do not appear in the government's budget figure. They are cloaked in what I would now call off-off-budget costs—those required of the private sector to comply with federal regulations.

The clearest example of why the cost should be budgeted is the economic impact on individual citizens of environmental regulation of electric utilities. The massive costs of smokestack scrubbers go directly to the consumer, the people who pay the bills for the product. Scrubbers do not in any way enhance the supply of electricity; they merely add to the cost with the objective of protecting the environment. If government could put scrubbers on all the utilities in the country, we could have devised the system, spent the money, and collected it back in taxes. Instead, we tell the utilities to put scrubbers on, and since the utilities operate on the monopoly system, we let them pass the cost on to the consumer in the way of a direct tax that is called part of the utility bill.

The federal government fails to show those higher prices. It also fails to show the higher prices resulting from economic regulation of interstate commerce, from federal air and safety standards. The costs and benefits of those social and commercial regulations should be more clearly disclosed both to the public and to the members of Congress when they make the decision. I specify disclosing the benefits, too, because they clearly exist. If the private-sector compliance costs were minor, their omission from the budget would not be a serious problem. They are not minor, however—they are significant and growing.

To control these regulatory costs, the Congressional Budget Act of 1974 should be amended to require Congress to establish annually a regulatory budget along with the fiscal budget to set a limit on the cost of compliance that each agency can lay on the rest of society, private and public sectors both. That should be done along with the fiscal budget so that the Budget Committee and Congress would have a full measure of what government requirements are costing the individual citizen or corporate entities. The timetable and process for developing a regulatory budget under my bill, H.R. 76, would be similar to the procedures used in enacting the fiscal budget concurrent resolutions. A regulatory budget would, in addition, provide an incentive for regulatory agencies not only to limit their compliance costs, but also to be more conscious of the costs' existence.

It would have other important effects as well. A regulatory budget along with a fiscal budget would provide a more accurate picture of the government's total impact on the economy, allowing Congress to determine how much of the nation's output will be directed by government and how much will be directed by the private sector. It would make possible a better balance between regulatory programs and the traditional method by which the government has acted in these areas—that is, direct spending on the objectives they want to reach. It would enhance the protection of the public's health and safety by requiring that the federal government establish consistent priorities in pursuing regulatory objectives.

I recognize that measuring compliance costs is a difficult problem. Such measurements are in an early stage of evolution, but I am very optimistic. Since 1970 there have been a number of cost estimates of federal regulation—the Office of Management and Budget study in 1974, the Council of Economic Advisers in 1976, a purchasing agency study in 1978, and also in 1978 the Paperwork Commission study. These estimates range from $100 to $120 billion. A recent study by Arthur Andersen and Company for the Business Roundtable takes a different approach from that of the other studies. This was a microstudy on the investment costs and paperwork costs and the changes in production costs and operating and administrative costs that were required of forty-eight companies by the regulations of six federal agencies. The studies illustrate that work is being done, and the spur of proposed legislation will intensify the efforts.

We should crank up our computers, put our best brains to work, and try to figure the cost before the government does things like the Clean Air Act. We do not have to have a comprehensive figure of all costs to implement the regulatory budget. We do not have to include the secondary costs, such as productivity losses, resource misallocation, and so forth. We should be aware of those costs, of course, and be thinking about them, but as long as each agency operates under the same ground rules and the universe of costs is carefully defined, there should be no problem. The year-to-year changes in cost are really the important consideration. Beginning with a practical and carefully defined cost universe, Congress can set regulatory ceilings. The yearly changes in regulations must be kept within bounds by the regulatory budget concurrent resolutions.

Congress and the executive branch should begin now to work out the methods necessary to make a regulatory budget a reality in the very near future. Enactment of H.R. 76 is the first step. A regulatory budget will encourage government agencies to develop cost-effective regulations. It will supplement the annual fiscal budget to give the public, Congress, the president, the investor, everybody, a comprehensive view of the federal government's command over resources and, above all, its impact on our society.

Can a Regulatory Budget Be Calculated?

Ralph Nader

The regulatory budget, as a relatively new introduction among ways to paralyze government, should bear the burden of proof. I propose to ask, Why is a regulatory budget needed?

The present regulatory process uses both quantitative and judgmental criteria in issuing standards, determining recalls, and fostering research and development. These criteria are intended to advance certain economic policies and—what is more and more significant in the new agencies—to advance the rights of health and safety of the American people, whether in the environment, the marketplace, or on the job. It is unfortunate, but true, that it is very difficult to measure human lives in dollars, although we in fact do that in various decisions, not so much by the computer as by judgment and intuition.

For example, if we sent two astronauts into orbit and they suddenly had trouble, I doubt that anybody would deny the cost-benefit of a $2 billion rescue effort. Indeed, we have developed a judgmental evaluation of loss of human life on a vertical scale. Traditionally, the cheapest loss of human life has been underground; second, on the highway; third, in the air; and fourth, in orbit. It seems the farther one gets from the earth, the more society is willing to spend in saving one's life.

Exchanging dollars for health and safety cannot be reduced to a formula; it cannot be reduced to a specific umbrella or ceiling, like a regulatory budget; and it certainly cannot be handled through intricate intrusion into the regulatory process by Congress, which already has its hands full trying to deal with the major policy issues and directions of the nation.

It is because of these considerations that the administrative process was set up some decades ago under the Administrative Procedures Act and, even before that, under established procedures for issuing standards. Regulatory behavior is subject to due process of law. The standards are proposed; there is a public hearing or an open docket; interested parties make their comments; and the agency, after some time, issues the standards. The interested parties can appeal to the courts, which have been known to overthrow standards they considered arbitrary and capricious. On occasion, the Congress can initiate legislation to change the whole process, as it did recently with the Civil Aeronautics Board.

Given these three basic regulatory stages—the internal appeal, the judicial stage, and the legislative stage—where is the problem? We often hear that there is a problem. Congressman Brown comments on the size of the *Code of Federal Regulations* and how it has grown from umpteen thousand pages in 1970 to umpteen-umpteen thousand pages now. If that is the level of the analysis used to justify the regulatory budget, it seems rather questionable. The *Code of Federal Regulations* has had a typographical change making the type larger and the margins smaller. Many of its pages are given over to standards for the protection of privacy and to regulations dealing with investment tax credits. The whole corporate subsidy effort certainly enlarges the *Code of Federal Regulations* as well. Its size is a very rough measure of regulation. Even those pages that are devoted to regulation reflect the hammer blows of companies who want exemptions and waivers and the companies' lawyers who want to work in Washington so they can continue to expand their operations.

Where, then, is the problem? The problem is that there is not nearly enough regulation. The National Highway Traffic Safety Administration, between 1969 and 1981, will have issued not one significant standard. The first significant regulation will be the passive restraints standard, effective in the fall of 1981 and applying only to large cars. The history of the Federal Trade Commission, until its new leadership, has been somewhere between limbo and slumber. The Occupational Safety and Health Administration under Nixon and Ford moved at a snail's pace, if that, and part of its activity was to withhold standards and sanctions to facilitate reelection of the president in 1972. Internal memoranda released after the Watergate tragedy pointed that out.

Inadequate regulation and law enforcement extend to almost every agency. OSHA has done very little about the most serious goals of regulation; carcinogens are just beginning to be dealt with. Many of the so-called regulations OSHA has published, like the shape of a toilet bowl and the size of a ladder, came directly from industry trade standards—verbatim. OSHA's priorities were indeed distorted by the philosophies current in the White House.

It is also ignored that many potential regulations can oppose inflation, help lessen the problem of getting value for the consumer dollar. Automobile repair fraud costs $15 to $18 billion a year, but very little has been done to regulate the industry. Indeed, the White House economists are always very eager to slow down or weaken proposed standards, but they have never once, in our experience, told an agency to speed up or make more stringent a proposed standard because it will make for a fairer marketplace, a more competitive marketplace, or more value for consumers' dollars in these inflationary times.

Much of the basis for a regulatory budget comes from a few studies, such as Murray Weidenbaum's. If that study had been conducted by a student in economics, I would flunk him. Weidenbaum starts out with the agencies' direct appropriations. He then takes a rather arbitrary multiple—twenty times—to get his figure of $100 billion a year. He does not consider benefits, which is like concluding that a company cost consumers $30 billion last year without indicating what products they received in exchange.

There are even more problems with his methodology in other studies. For example, in the automobile safety budgets, he included the grant-in-aid programs to each state. Then he multiplied that by twenty. That can really add up. He also included the cost of the seatbelt interlock, even though it was repealed several years ago—and he multiplied that by twenty. Finally, he relied on industry cost figures unquestioningly, even though anybody who studies the history of alleged costs of regulation to big business knows these figures are very often wildly inflated.

The chemical industry reacted to the vinyl chloride standard by issuing a statement that it would cause the loss of 2 million jobs and an economic loss of $60 to $90 billion. The standard was issued—one of the few times the government called an industry's bluff—and no jobs were lost. Indeed, one or two of the companies said by changing their procedures they actually became more efficient. This brings us to the basic issue of costs: whether economists have the tools to deal with them and whether Congress, in setting policy, can reflect the inadequacy of those tools.

How do we calculate direct and indirect costs? Whose costs do we take, the industry's costs or consumers' costs? If we take the industry's cost, should we have a requirement that eliminates the trade secret barrier to cost disclosure? How else can we rely on the veracity of the figures when there is a conflict of interest? Industry wants, of course, to defeat the regulation. On the other hand, it wants to have its cost figures accepted. The automobile industry has been notorious for exaggerating costs, as we have shown every time we could get internal computer printouts (for the seatbelt–shoulder harness, for example).

That is not the only question. The other problem, besides the trade secret barrier, in verifying industry costs concerns such private companies as mismanaged Chrysler. Moreover, should we also have a set-aside for bribes that are costing companies so much money, or should we take the cost in the isolated context as reflected by the company?

Then there is the subsidy question. The government is full of subsidies to big business—tax exemptions, agribusiness subsidies, maritime subsidies, aviation subsidies, the license or protection-from-competition subsidies, tariffs, and so on. Are subsidies to be considered part of the regulatory budget because they have a regulatory impact? The Price-Anderson Act, for example, is subsidizing the nuclear power industry. It also has a regulatory effect in telling millions of people in the range of a nuclear meltdown that they cannot collect compensation for damage done to them to the full limits of assets of nuclear power companies.

Certainly, loan guarantees have a regulatory impact. They say to credit seekers who are not under the loan guarantee umbrella that they will be at a disadvantage in getting credit from banks. Tax exemptions, of course, have a severe regulatory effect, and they also have a strong lobby. Are we going to include them or exclude them?

The question also involves time span, particularly for amortization. If investment to meet a certain health and safety standard is a one-year or two-year cost, how many years of benefits should we compare it with? This, of course, is another matter of judgment. It is not a matter Congress seems to be able to handle on a case-by-case program, which is why they set up regulatory agencies rather than legislate each standard in the first place.

The Department of Commerce, commenting on the Office of Management and Budget's proposal for a regulatory budget, has apparently come to a substantial consensus that the economic tools needed for an analysis of the regulatory process do not exist. The cost of compliance, too, is a whole hornet's nest. For instance, an industry can increase the cost of a standard by delaying it. Airbag standards were delayed, and airbags now cost more than they would have had they been required in 1974–1975, when the president of General Motors, standing alone in the industry, called for them.

There is also the question of emergencies. Suppose Congress sets a regulatory budget for EPA, saying, "This is all you can inflict on the perpetrators of health and safety hazards in the next year." Suddenly, in the middle of the year, a great explosion of concern arises about asbestos poisoning of children in schools. What is EPA going to do? It will either have to squeeze other meritorious efforts out or go to Congress for a supplement, which will probably run into a filibuster by the Orrin Hatches of the Congress.

These questions are not intended simply to point out the difficulties of a regulatory budget in our political and economic and constitutional system. They are meant to indicate that the burden of proof is not on the people who want to continue the present system, which has suffered from too little regulation, from too few recalls, from too little information to the consumer, from too little resistance to monopolistic practices, from too much indifference. The burden of proof is on those who propose the regulatory budget. Those in Congress who favor it should analyze how it is going to change Congress. How much of a cost and time load can Congress take? How much more special pleading by campaign financers around this or that standard?

It is very important in our quest for monetary precision, I might add, to consider the one area in which government is trying to defend the broader public interest rather than to serve business and industrial needs, which makes up the bulk of its activity. We have been very careful about making pronouncements that put a dollar value on human life. But we should ask ourselves, is not the loss of human life the greatest dollar inefficiency? Are not disease and contaminated water the greatest inefficiencies? Are not the damages radiation inflicts on our genetic inheritance for millions of years the greatest inefficiencies? If we cannot empathize with the victims, perhaps we should spend some time in our foundries and factories and mines to get a feeling for them. The president and his associates, including the board of directors, of Armco Steel went down one day into the mines underground, and one of them said: "After thirty minutes down there I could not straighten up. It was dark. It was damp. And I will never again say the coal miners are overpaid."

Reasonable Aims through Reasonable Means

Irving Kristol

I do not plan to discuss in any detail the pros and cons of specific structures or processes involved in a regulatory budget. I am neither a sophisticated legislator nor a sophisticated lobbyist. I report my opinions simply because they might reflect those of "the folks way out there." Simply put, my view is that regulation has gotten out of hand, and something must be done to bring it under control.

My favorite horror story concerns a low-income housing project in New York City where construction was suspended for some four months while the Environmental Protection Agency insisted the buildings be redesigned to cope with noise pollution. This housing was for people living in slums where they were being bitten by rats, where there was no heat or hot water, and where ceilings were crumbling. One would have thought that noise pollution was the last thing in the world they were worried about. Nevertheless, EPA won its battle. The buildings were redesigned, and now the cost of a four-room apartment in low-income housing in New York, which used to be $45,000, is $75,000. Government regulation is not entirely responsible for the cost, but it is responsible for a substantial portion of the increase. There is something wrong when the government builds housing for low-income people but at the same time imposes regulations that price it out of their market.

Putting the issue in a broader perspective, the regulatory budget addresses the question, Do we want a fifth branch of government? Some of us are still getting used to the fourth branch, the media. We are accepting it, however: it is one of those constitutional changes that, while no one was prepared for it, may yet work out for the better. Still, we think it precipitate at the moment to add a fifth branch of government. That is going too fast. Those who argue against the regulatory budget have come down in favor of a set of independent agencies, a set of independent overseers. Some are now arguing in the courts that the agencies ought to be free of executive interference, as they are already free to a large extent of congressional interference. One of these days they may even get free of judicial interference.

In the absence of a regulatory budget, these agencies have, in effect, an infinite budget—not in terms of congressional appropriations, which is the least of it, but in the sense that they have a nearly unlimited freedom to mandate costs upon the private sector. There is no limit by law to the costs they can require. The idea behind the regulatory budget is that someone should set a limit. It makes no sense to allow these agencies that extraordinary power of taxation, which is what the costs they mandate amount to.

What we have developed in this country—unwittingly, I would like to think—is a regulatory establishment with the power to tax the American people arbitrarily and to an unlimited extent. One might argue that the tax is on business, not on the people. But there is no such thing as a tax on business. Taxes on business are taxes on the workers, on the consumers, or on the stockholders. Business corporations are economic mechanisms. Taxes placed on these mechanisms are simply transferred out.

In short, "we out there" feel that regulation must be made more reasonable and that the regulatory budget seems to be an appropriate mechanism for doing so. Mr. Nader points out the difficulties of getting the appropriate cost figures, but the existence of differences of opinion regarding costs and benefits does not mean that we cannot estimate them at all. Obviously we should; obviously we must.

One of the most striking things about regulation is the difference between Europe and the United States. The comparison leads one to all sorts of malicious speculations, or seemingly malicious speculations, about the motives behind the drive in this country for ever greater regulation. The kinds of government regulation that exist in Europe are far more reasonable, less oppressive, and less expensive than those in the United States. This is true even under socialist governments—the Labor government in Britain, the Social Democratic government in Germany, and the long-standing Socialist government in Sweden. This does cause one to wonder.

The explanation, I believe, is very simple. I never thought I would live to regret the absence in the United States of a socialist party, but I begin to think more and more these days that we may really be missing something. One of the problems created by the absence of a socialist party is that all those political energies and political ideas that normally go into such a party go in this country, where socialism is not respectable, into movements, such as the environmentalist movement or the movement for greater government regulation. In Europe, precisely because there are large, legitimate socialist parties that at some point have to govern, the attitude toward regulation is far more responsible. No socialist party in Europe wants to wreck the economy. It is their economy.

They will have to make it work at some point, because at some point they, as the official opposition, will be in office.

Here in the United States, the regulatory impulse seems to be directed against the economy itself. That is, the people who are demanding ever greater regulation, ever greater governmental interference in the economy, the piling of more and more costs on business activity, are not the people who will someday have to make the economy work. They are not the people who will be held responsible for economic growth or its absence. There is in this division of labor in the United States a built-in irresponsibility on the part of those who are arguing for more and more regulation.

I repeat. visit the countries in Europe, especially those with socialist governments, and you will discover that their regulations are much more reasonable, more cost conscious, and more sophisticated in their application of cost-benefit analysis than ours. The only reason I can think of for this is that socialists in Europe do take responsibility for the economy. Regulators in this country do not. The regulators, or regulationists—choose whichever term you wish—seem to think that there is a difference between something called business and something called the economy, that you can attack business but not damage the economy. That only makes sense within the socialist context, when you are prepared to have government take the place of business. In the context of our society, business is the economy. To the degree that we injure one, we injure the other.

The adversary impulse among regulationists can be destructive in a way that the pure and open socialist impulse in Europe need not be. We cannot afford to have our economy mindlessly destroyed in this way. To the degree that we have government regulation—and it is quite obvious that we need it and that we will have it—we must have some way of estimating the reasonable costs and the reasonable benefits obtained from specific modes.

This is not easy, as Mr. Nader has pointed out. But the problems can be solved. They require that reasonable government try to achieve reasonable aims through reasonable means. I refuse to believe the American government is incapable of that. I find that Mr. Nader shows a shocking distrust in the integrity and the ability of our government to do, really, a very simple thing, namely, to reach certain broad conclusions about what the economic burdens of regulation should be for a particular period of time. And that is what "we folks out there" think.

Summary of Discussion

In the discussion that followed the presentations on a regulatory budget, questions arose about the relationship between this concept and the application of cost-benefit analysis. Congressmen Brown emphasized that weighing benefits and costs should be distinguished from simply choosing the "cheapest" regulatory approach. He also noted that, while the regulatory budget would not itself include estimates of benefits, that is also true of the fiscal budget. In his view, Congress could make broad judgments on priorities in the absence of explicit benefit estimates for regulation as it does with the fiscal budget. He also emphasized the need for analysis of benefits, particularly in making judgments about particular regulatory proposals.

The other major topic discussed was the extent to which current procedures on the regulatory budget were conducive to balanced treatment in regulatory decision making. Congressman Brown argued that favoring a budget did not imply being against spending. Who makes decisions on health and safety issues must not be overlooked, according to Mr. Nader. If they are not made by government (under regulations), they are made by corporations. Moreover, in his view, the current process has merit, business has conceded that regulation has had favorable effects, and the costs have not proved to be excessive, particularly in light of the human lives at stake. Mr. Kristol noted that "human lives are always at stake" and that while this makes the issues somewhat difficult to discuss without appearing to be lacking in compassion, we make choices in recognition of this fact in all our economic, social, and leisure activities.

Part Five

The Case-by-Case Approach to Regulatory Reform

Introduction

Robert J. Samuelson, Chairman

Regulatory reform is simply a new euphemism for politics: it is a struggle of ideas and interests, and in the end the winners win because they have superior firepower. But what does that mean?

This section explores the pragmatic political aspects of regulatory change—not who is right so much as who wins and why. Like all politics, each episode of combat is different, but certain generalities apply to almost all regulatory politics.

First, virtually every regulatory scheme—no matter how good or how bad—creates vested interests. There are the regulators themselves. Usually, but not always, they favor continued and expanded regulation, because their jobs are at stake and because, if they attempt to do their jobs well, they are bound to rationalize their work by justifying its desirability. To be sure, in the last half of the 1970s a number of agencies—the Civil Aeronautics Board, the Interstate Commerce Commission, and the Federal Communications Commission—took steps to loosen the regulations they had long defended and enforced. But every bureaucracy has an instinct for self-preservation. As often as not, the impetus for change was not spontaneous: once Congress begins pushing for change, regulatory agencies become remarkably flexible and adaptive. This is not to say that all change is motivated only by a self-interested desire to stay in business. Individual instances of regulatory change are often due to key new appointees, who are not tied to past practices and whose commitment to change appears genuine. But their appointment is usually part of the basic political process. They do not arrive on the scene accidentally.

In addition to the regulators themselves, virtually every agency has important constituencies that favor what it does and want regulation to be preserved. In some cases, the regulated industries are the main constituencies. Airlines and truckers, for example, traditionally opposed deregulation of their industries. Although they were often unhappy with specific rulings, they believed by and large that they benefited by the pattern of commerce created by regulation and feared the uncertainty that would follow a massive liberalization. But the major constituencies are not always the regulated industries. The main supporting constituency for the Environmental Protection Agency is the mass of environmental groups; for the Federal Trade Commission, it consists of consumer groups.

No matter what the supporting constituencies are, they are likely to have allies in specialized congressional committees and subcommittees and in batteries of lawyers, consultants, and economists—including, often, ex-regulators and ex-legislators—whose livelihoods and sense of self-esteem are wrapped up in the regulatory process. All these forces become engaged in any effort at "regulatory reform."

Second, winning is not simply a matter of constituency size. Regulatory politics is a contest of *both* interests and ideas. At the beginning of the 1970s, environmentalists could not be seriously considered an imposing political interest group. They were numerous, but they were not well organized. Moreover, they faced business lobbying groups that—if not as awesome as their critics contend—had maintained a considerable presence in Washington for decades. The triumph of the environmental movement and the enactment of some of its key goals into legislation were due to the popularity of its central ideas—that the environment was an essential part of the nation's living standards and that business, left to itself, would waste this national asset—and to the inability of business to offer an effective counterargument. As the environmental movement became increasingly better organized in the 1970s, it also suffered setbacks. Again, ideas were at play. Business was able to convince many legislators that environmentalists' goals often resulted in staggering costs without corresponding benefits.

Politics, in the popular view, is often "dirty," the game going to the side that can best play on legislators' need for money or for electoral support. It is less fashionable to think that legislators sometimes simply strive to do what they honestly believe is in the public interest. In fact, that is often what happens, and the evidence of this section—all from veterans of skirmishes of regulatory reform—is that the combatants are well aware of this reality. Uniformly, they believe that "making their case" is a vital part of the political process.

Finally—and this truth applies to much of legislative and administrative politics—the substance of change is often critically involved in details known or understood by relatively small numbers of people. This aspect of regulatory change does not emerge distinctly from the evidence of this section, but it is worth remembering. Public officials, whether elected or appointed, love to embrace popular ideas. Indeed, their enthusiasm is usually so great that they will happily embrace four or five conflicting ideas in one breath. The nation's laws are littered with legislative preambles that create mutually exclusive or contradictory objectives for public policy.

It is here that the skill of the players becomes vital. Their ability to manipulate details, either in regulations or in legislation, can have a profound effect on the real economic impact of regulatory policies. It is always important to watch not only what Congress or a regulatory agency says it is doing but also—two or three years later—what actually happened in the real world. That is where the winning and losing really occur.

Reform by the
Civil Aeronautics Board

Elizabeth E. Bailey

I would like to review the emergence of regulatory reform from within the Civil Aeronautics Board and then focus on the events following passage of the Airline Deregulation Act.

When Alfred Kahn and I arrived at the CAB during the summer of 1977, the idea of reform in aviation had strong political support. Senators Edward Kennedy and Howard Cannon had already drafted a bill, and the Carter administration had strongly endorsed reform. Dr. Kahn and I had the job of implementing that reform—providing a period during which, before the passage of the reform legislation, Congress would be able to see what a reform-minded board could do. When Dr. Kahn came in, he was committed to reform but seemed to be not quite as fast a reformer as President Carter was. During his first few months, there were two major decisions, both involving international air policy, in which the president adopted more procompetitive policies than the CAB. One case involved low rates from New York to London; the other had to do with opening up interior routes in the United States and selecting carriers most likely to force prices down across the Atlantic.

Dr. Kahn soon took the leadership in speedy implementation of procompetitive policies. Within two or three months, he, I, and the new people he had brought to lead the staff adopted a strategy of doing everything we could to bring about domestic reform. With regard to pricing, our policy was to approve in a pro forma fashion all discount tariffs brought before us. At the same time, we instituted a more long-range strategy for price flexibility. The board expedited treatment of cases involving carriers that promised lower fares and used low fares as a criterion for decision in seeking carriers to serve markets.

With regard to entry, the board's 1977–1978 program reflected the belief that market forces were more likely to result in an economically rational initial and continuing selection of carriers than the CAB could hope to achieve with its traditional regulatory mechanism. Our ability to take a large immediate step in this direction was circumscribed, however. We started where we could, therefore, by liberalizing entry restrictions and introducing expedited procedures wherever possible.

In international policy, the board and the State Department took the lead in coming up with the liberal bilateral agreements that permitted more low prices and new low-fare services.

By the summer of 1978, the CAB's actions over the previous year had begun to bear fruit. Airline profits were hitting record levels because of a healthy economy and because of the success of the discount fares in filling empty seats on planes. Dr. Kahn was stunningly effective in publicizing the gains from our pricing policies—both for consumers and for carriers—and he enthusiastically communicated the reform message to Congress. A synergy began to appear between the agency carrying out reform and Congress. It was important that Congress knew the persons who were going to be conducting reform and had observed their successes. They were able to pass a bill supporting not just reform but deregulation.

In the administration of the deregulation bill, we are finding the issue of entry the easiest to deal with. Since the bill passed in October 1978, we have given out approximately five hundred routes under our certificate authority and a few hundred more under the dormant authority provisions of the act. New nonstop service has been instituted on several hundred of these routes. We have also continued the process of removing restrictions on carriers' operating authority, starting in the smaller communities and working up to larger ones. We intend systematically to remove all such restrictions.

In pricing, the zone of downward fare flexibility that the board had put in was almost identical with the one in the act. We are probably not going to grant additional pricing flexibility for another year or more, particularly with respect to joint fares, because we are eager to put the small community program into operation before we make another major change in price policy. Policies for the small community program are being designed now; indeed, we have gone all across the country to seek community input for it.

Another side to the deregulation story, besides entry, is exit. A number of communities have been having a difficult problem with decreased service during our transition under the act. We are doing the same kind of detailed study that Stephen G. Breyer did during the oversight hearings. One of the things we find from a case-by-case look is that, for instance, while Providence dropped 10 percent in service in the early months after deregulation, nearby Hartford had a 20 percent increase. We have been carefully monitoring the gains as well as the losses in small community service. We will be working over the coming months to administer the transition problems of exit as soundly as we can.

The final aspect of the transition will have to do with personnel. The CAB is beginning to lose some of its best midlevel lawyers. We will also have to manage the problems that some of the older staff may have in finding new jobs. Certainly, we will try to administer the transition so as to keep as many good and smart people at the board for as long as we can and to attract people eager to help set a precedent for going out of business in style.

We will also have to explore the transfer of some of our functions to other agencies. As an example, the CAB's consumer protection division is exploring possibilities with the Federal Trade Commission to move over, possibly before that is mandated to happen.

From this experience, I believe that one of the best ways to administer reform is to set a future date at which a reform will take place, giving both the agency and the industry a chance to make a transition. It is also advantageous if various functions do not end at the same time. Our authority over routes disappears two and a half years from now; our authority over rates disappears three and a half years from now; our authority over the small community program does not disappear for an additional five years. By having this variety of dates for our authorities to cease, particularly by having route authority cease before pricing authority, we can gather forces and plan for an orderly transition. I am finding, and I believe the other board members and the industry are finding, too, that phasing out is a much better way to make changes than to do everything suddenly.

The Lessons of
Airline Deregulation

Stephen G. Breyer

We need at this point a framework for accomplishing meaningful regulatory reform within which we can evaluate the various proposals. People have always been talking about the need for regulatory reform. The first proposal was probably in 1881, since the Interstate Commerce Commission was founded in 1880. Over the last thirty or forty years, most proposals have fallen into one of four categories: changing the procedures, changing the structure, changing personnel, and changing the substance, that is, the basic approach to regulating the substantive problem. I favor the fourth category, and I see serious flaws in the first three.

The flaw of the procedural approach is that it is highly technical. It is wonderful for lawyers. There may be only fifteen people in the country who really understand the history of a particular procedural provision. Maybe there are 1,500, but it is still a small number. In addition, it is not clear at all what the outcome of a procedural change will be in the real world. The bottom line is whether prices go down, whether there is greater health or safety, whether there is protection for the environment—reform will not be achieved by additional or changed procedure.

Imagine a bill that attempts reform by, for example, applying a separation-of-function requirement to rule making. That sounds rather good, but not many people know the implication of applying separation-of-function procedures in rule making. In fact, it has to do with whether the commissioners' staff people may or may not talk to experts within the agency about a "fact in issue" when they are preparing the opinion. Perhaps something really turns on this procedural change, but we are not quite certain what. We also suspect it varies from agency to agency, and it may well change over time. Thus we see Douglas Costle today at the Environmental Protection Agency supporting a bill that would apply separation-of-function provisions to formal or informal rule making, while at the same time, in *Hercules* v. *EPA*, the agency argues that it would be impossible to administer the Toxic Substances Control Act if its staff really had to abide by separation-of-function provisions.

With regard to this kind of reform, I suspect (1) that the effect in the world of changing procedures will be unpredictable; (2) that the effect will vary quite a lot; (3) that different groups of public interest lawyers and private interest groups will become very involved because they will see some tangential relationship to something they are substantially interested in. Procedural proposals will generate lots of heat but really not much light.

Their outcome, too, is likely to change over time. It is popular to say that it is a bad thing for the White House to intervene in the work of agencies because many fear they may interfere with effective environmental regulation. Yet how would we have felt thirty years ago when the agency in question was the Department of Defense or the Department of State, which were abandoning liberals because they were suspected of having been communists? In this situation, a little intervention along the lines of "Let's be less political and pay more attention to the merits" would have been welcome indeed. Reactions to procedures change over the years, and it is difficult for me to believe we can really have substantive reform through this approach. Procedural reforms are often good in their own right, but we should be careful of placing too much reliance on them.

The second kind of proposal is to revamp agency structure. The Advisory Council on Executive Organization illustrates this, saying we should give all power to the chairmen or restrict the commissions' independence by making them responsible to the president. Others want to go the other way. Philip Elman, a member of the Federal Trade Commission, argued several years ago that the way to reform that agency was to have less powerful chairmen. Of course, he thought that because he was not liked by the chairman. This kind of example reinforces my skepticism about making progress through the structural approach.

Then what can we do? Many people say we need better personnel. No one is more sympathetic in general to that than an academician. People are appointed to these commissions by the president on the advice of his staff or others. I would bet there has never been a suggestion such as, "You should appoint Jones—he is a really mediocre person." Recommendations are not made in that form; rather, the president hears from the appointing authorities that their nominee is a truly good person, highly qualified, indeed superb. The difficulty is in finding out who *are* the good people. What does that really mean, and how do we tell in advance? If we could find a foolproof selection process, or even a better selection process, we could solve a lot of problems, not just in regulation.

My predilection is for the substantive approach, which is what we took with the Civil Aeronautics Board. I would like to discuss that experience and raise some questions in an attempt to be provocative.

One thing seemed absolutely certain at the outset: we would never get reform of airline regulation. The industry was against it. The unions were against it. Nobody cared about it. The only people who would benefit were a few travelers, who are only the richer people in the country. The business traveler did not need it. It seemed the least likely thing imaginable even to try. In 1974 we did try, and with many people's cooperation, got results. Perhaps we were just lucky, but perhaps something is due to the way we approached the problem.

One lesson of the experience is that far more than either my associates in the academic world or those in government would have thought depended on a thorough, detailed, and absolutely nonprejudiced study of the issue. This was an issue that many thought had been studied to death, but in fact it had not. This time Congress and those in charge of policy wanted to know what would happen in the world, not what a theory said.

If PSA flies for $18 from San Francisco to Los Angeles but Boston to Washington costs $42, it sounds as if the more competitive system in California is the right one. But the airlines argued that the difference was due to the weather or to more expensive personnel, higher load capacity, differences in air congestion, and so on. Only when you look deeply into each of those arguments and draw together all the facts do you convince people that the initial reaction was correct. It was the competition in California that brought lower fares. Theory alone is not convincing. The more detailed the study, the better.

Hearings serve in this respect as a catalyst for those who have the information to produce it. For example, the major argument against deregulation in air transport, as in trucks, was that small towns would lose service. This is a good argument with members of Congress, particularly if they come from such towns. We were more persuasive in this regard, however, because we went to United Airlines, sat with the vice-president, and went through their computer printouts line by line, route by route, segment by segment, asking which ones would be discontinued. They started out by saying 350, including the route from Kennedy Airport to Newark. Finally, we reached agreement on a number—29—that accounted for 0.1 percent of the total revenue passenger-miles flown. At that point, when we could show that a very small amount of small town service would be affected, we could be far more persuasive with Congress and other policy makers.

The second lesson I learned is the importance of presenting details and examples in the hearing so that people can understand the process and write about it in the newspapers. That may be overemphasized in

Washington, but a report not presented through dramatic examples will just go on the shelf. Publicity is needed to convince people who are in the middle and who really want to do the right thing. The examples, therefore, should not only be dramatic; they should also reveal something of underlying importance.

A great moment in our hearings came when the CAB said it had no route moratorium. A policy that prevented carriers from getting new routes was unlawful and not one they were prepared to admit they had. We produced a memorandum from administrative law judge Ralph Wiser: "The following cases which have been set for hearing have been taken off the hearing docket under informal instructions from the chairman's office pursuant to the route moratorium." And the chairman had just said there was no route moratorium. This was a very dramatic effect, a lawyer's delight, and something people write about; but it was also enlightening. The underlying reason they canceled the hearings was that they were desperately trying to stop too many planes from flying. Why? Because the planes were flying half empty. Why? Because the board had stopped price competition, and without price competition travelers have to fly on planes that are 40 percent full and pay fares that are twice as high as they need to be. Stopping flights was a restrictive form of regulation—it was classic service rate making. This dramatic example showed up a basic flaw in the system.

I am arguing two things. The first is that the substantive, agency-by-agency approach offers the best hope of real change, and one of the reasons for that is the importance of detail that you can only get in this way. The second is the importance of thorough study guided by an overall framework and filled with dramatic examples that will interest the press, and therefore the public, and begin to arouse the constituency that always exists for meaningful change. That is what we did with the CAB, with the help of the Ford and Carter administrations, members of the board itself, and two chairmen. It required a lot of time and effort, but it has been reasonably successful.

Deregulation in the Trucking Industry: A Small Carrier's View

Harold H. Shay

I am one of the people in the trucking business who make up the 15,000 or so carriers that no one seems to know about. My company, which is family owned, was founded by my father. My two sons and I hope it will survive at least another generation. Many people concerned with regulatory policy could probably name only a handful of motor carriers that they believe do most of the business in the industry, but the existence of so many of us small and medium carriers dispels the myth that there is no competition. Between Buffalo and Rochester, which are about seventy miles apart, we had at last count thirty-five competitors.

It is very difficult for me to understand why the bureaucracy is tinkering with a system that is working so well. I favor regulation, and I would like to put into proper perspective the heart of the motor carrier question.

Clearly, we must have a motor carrier system. Airlines and railroads serve very limited corridors; when they come to the end, their cargo must go to a motor carrier. The same is true of water transport. With few exceptions, no commodity shipment is originated and terminated without the involvement of a motor truck.

Advocates of airline deregulation are celebrating, but those who are not so sure are taking a wait-and-see attitude. In discussions of airline deregulation, such New York cities as Utica, Corning, and Elmira are referred to as small, but to those of us in the motor carrier business these places are not small; they are crucial to the American enterprise system. Motor carriers serve every crossroad and hamlet in the United States, with routes and joint rates to 50,000 communities.

Senator Kennedy is concerned about the ills of the collective rate-making process. I have invited him to come to Dansville, New York, which is our home office, where he can learn that it is impossible to operate a motor carrier system without collective rate making and immunity from the antitrust laws. I have come to the conclusion that if we could change the name of the Interstate Commerce Commission to the Motor Carrier Transportation User Protective Agency, put the correct bureaus under its jurisdiction, and double its budget, we would solve much of what seems to be a problem. As a small carrier, I must defend ICC. Without it and the collective rate-making process, there would be no system of transportation. Certainly, there would be trucks, more and more of them—and less and less efficiency.

Deregulation, in my opinion, means this: unstable prices, lower in some areas but higher in most; lower quality of service; more trucks, and who needs more trucks? We have the responsibility to see that those that already traverse our highways are used efficiently. May I suggest that we think of the motor carrier transportation system as the circulatory system of the human body. We are pumping out commerce and industry through the veins and arteries of the system. There are big ones and little ones, and we must view the system in its totality. We cannot compare it with perhaps 2,000 jet airliners serving 600 communities that make up the American air system. Tinkering with the circulatory system will certainly stop circulation to parts of the business and industrial body, hastening its decay. This country in the last thirty years has had a great thing happen: we have created a great industrial compound for all the forty-eight United States. We should not compare our system with Canada's or Sweden's; we must compare the United States with what we had before regulation and what we would have without it. I must say I do not understand the urge to deregulate air and rail transportation because they are doing so poorly, but to deregulate the trucking industry because we are doing so well.

Those who have influence over the direction of regulatory reform must understand that we small carriers are not against reform, but we say, Please, don't throw the baby out with the bath water. If we lose collective rate making, our system will come apart. If anyone is dreaming that it is a way to get at the strong labor movement, forget it. I am not in concert with Frank Fitzsimmons and the Teamsters; I abhor what goes on in that negotiation. But deregulation will give us, in place of the Teamsters Union, another group that will organize the independent truckers. The results will make the 1974 fuel stop look like a kindergarten exercise. This is because there is no more intimidating position for a small operator than to go to a large shipper to negotiate a level of rates that will assure it of the adequate and dependable business it needs. Are we willing to turn our highways into a holocaust? Those who have an influence on this must resist it.

The Process of Deregulation: Comparing the Airlines, Railroads, and Motor Carriers

John W. Snow

One of the fascinating features of the regulatory reform debate is the disparity between the efforts that go into reform and the results that come out of it. There is lots of activity, but there are few triumphs. Maybe that reflects the extent of the need, or maybe it reflects some misallocation of resources on the part of those of us who are advocating reform. We have been good at analyzing the deficiencies in regulatory statutes, good at analyzing the failings of regulatory programs, and good at coming up with reform proposals, but not very good at delivering results.

There are some exceptions, most notably airline deregulation, where we are seeing real-world results. It might be useful to reflect on some of the forces that produced the airline deregulation triumph and see what application they might have to the counterpart trucking and railroad cases that are now pending.

It is staggering to realize that the airline regulatory reform proposal went from conception to birth in less than four years. What accounts for it is obvious: an effective coalition. The Ford administration introduced a bill; it was followed by the Carter administration's attention to the issue; and Senator Kennedy, on the Administrative Practices and Procedures Subcommittee, gave the issue a great deal of public attention through hearings and through the study that Mr. Breyer has discussed. An effective coalition coalesced around both administrations, the Kennedy group, and the counterpart group in the House.

Economists had been arguing for years that aviation regulation is highly inefficient, but they had also been arguing for years that railroad and trucking regulation were highly inefficient. Yet we see the first appearance of regulatory reform in the airline industry, not in the rail or trucking industry. Why? The one major distinction between air transportation and the other two is the existence of a powerful, compelling idea with real-world evidence to support it—the idea that deregulation will lead air fares to fall without adverse consequences to safety, to service levels to the public, to investors, that is, to all the constituents of regulation. The evidence came from the experience in Texas and California, where in a less regulated environment we could observe air fares that were 30, 40, or 50 percent lower than on comparable interstate routes. When Senator Kennedy's hearings and Senator Cannon's hearings explored this in extensive detail, it turned out that the lines with lower fares were flying the same airplanes, they were paying comparable wage rates, their safety record was excellent, and small communities were getting service.

As these findings were made public through the Kennedy and Cannon hearings and through the press, the airlines found themselves on the defensive. How did they account for the fare differentials? They tried to account for them by pointing out the differences, but on close examination the differences did not explain them. We came back to the conclusion that intrastate air fares were lower because in a less regulated environment, with price competition, airlines operate more efficiently. People in the political process were comfortable with the idea because the deregulation of airlines meant public benefits without public risk. The legislation began to move and produced the result we see today.

When we turn to the railroads and the trucks, we see that the economists' case is made. The economists tell us that trucking has none of the characteristics of a public utility. It is an industry that would operate well in the mainstream of American business. It is, in fact, almost a prototype for an effective competitive industry. In the case of railroads, they tell us that continuing regulation is having devastating consequences because the railroad industry is tied in a straitjacket that has prevented it from adapting to the new competitive world since 1887, when railroads occupied a different role in commercial activity. Railroads are no longer monopolies, but they are treated that way. That destroys the vitality of the industry.

The Carter administration favors reform of truck and rail regulation. Hearings on rail reform are now pending in both houses of Congress. Senator Kennedy, chairman of the committee that is considering the issue, has said he will make it a priority. Coalitions are beginning to be formed. Debate is beginning to unfold. But in neither case do we have the nice, clear-cut comparison in the real world that shows us that the results in a less regulated environment are clearly superior without significant risk. Yes, there are some cases, such as the deregulation of poultry products twenty years ago, after which truck rates fell 30 percent. The ultimate consumer of poultry did not see any significant change in poultry prices, however. Shippers who buy trucking services are in a different position from the ultimate consumer. In the case of railroads, deregulation is likely to mean higher rates, and in some cases it will certainly mean some less service. This is a far less appealing case than could be made for the airlines industry.

Another factor may be even more significant, though. The other side of the economists' argument is inefficiency, which they use to argue against the continuation of regulation. That leads to the axiom the greater the inefficiency resulting from some regulatory system, the more difficult it is to get that system undone because it creates an enormous constituency. It includes the mill that operates at the end of an uneconomic branch line, the shipper that is now getting its costs subsidized, the trucking firm that has paid a large price for its certificates. In each of those cases, there is an identifiable inefficiency that is treated as an equity by someone who will take part in the political process.

I am suggesting that two things count. One is a good story, the effective and unassailable argument that makes people in the political process comfortable. The other is the height of the regulatory hurdle we have to jump. The greater the inefficiencies generated by the regulatory system, the higher that hurdle, that is, the larger the constituency that benefits from the regulatory system and the greater interest they have in preserving it.

Summary of Discussion

The discussion that followed the presentations on the case-by-case approach began with a question to Mr. Breyer: Does his framework for accomplishing regulatory reform apply to environmental and health and safety regulation as well as economic regulation, particularly since "social" regulation deals with such issues as valuation of human life? Mr. Breyer replied that substantive changes can and should be made in social as well as economic regulation and pointed to the "totally false dichotomy" of life versus dollars as an example of the need to reform the substantive basis of social regulatory programs. He noted that the decision to regulate or not is made on grounds of the risk of injury or death, not the life of a specific individual. Decisions are made to construct buildings, for example, even when it is known in advance that some percentage of construction workers will lose their lives.

A second questioner asked the panel to discuss the proposed legislative veto and sunset laws as they relate to the case-by-case approach. Ms. Bailey replied that sunset provisions give both agencies and businesses warning that change is coming and a chance to move in the direction of that change. Mr. Snow agreed and added that he is uncomfortable about legislative veto provisions. On the basis of his experience as administrator of the National Highway Traffic Safety Administration, he sees the legislative veto as a way of letting off political pressure when a regulatory agency exceeds political constraints and feels that it does not solve the deeper substantive problems. Mr. Breyer expressed misgivings about both the legislative veto and the sunset approach. Sunset, he said, leaves open the possibility that a small minority of legislators can act to kill a regulatory agency, and legislative veto provisions concentrate too much power in a single committee and encourage inappropriate intervention by Congress in nonpolicy matters. He suggested an alternative approach under which regulatory agencies are reviewed one by one over the course of several years on predetermined terms.

Part
Six

Cost-Benefit Analysis of Social
Regulation

Introduction

James C. Miller III, Chairman

Aside from energy, with its plethora of economic controls, the major increase in regulation during the past decade has been in the so-called social areas. By and large, the federal government's regulation of specific industries—such as transportation—has changed little in either scale or scope. There has been a mushrooming of federal involvement, however, in the areas of health, safety, and the environment. Several new agencies have been created—the Occupational Safety and Health Administration, the Environmental Protection Agency, and the Consumer Product Safety Commission, to name only three.

This newer type of regulation has two notable characteristics that are relevant here. First, its application to American industry is extremely broad. Virtually every establishment is covered by new occupational safety and health rules, companies that do not fall under some environmental regulations are few, and manufacturers of consumer products not only are now subject to liability laws but also may have to answer to a federal safety commission. In a sense, this new type of regulation is similar to the old type of economic regulation. Typically, beneficiaries of economic regulation have been the industries regulated (protected from competition), whereas those bearing the costs have been many and diffuse (ordinary consumers). The beneficiaries of social regulation are often relatively few (employees exposed to unsafe or unhealthful workplaces, "environmentalists," and those preferring a different, safer mix of consumer products), whereas those who bear the cost are many and relatively diffuse (again, many ordinary consumers). In both cases, it is at least arguable that the constituents have "captured" the agencies. With economic regulation, the regulated industries do the capturing; with social regulation, the industry's antagonists seem to have carried the day.

A second notable characteristic of this new wave of social regulation is the unusually high degree of emotional, moral, and ideological fervor that characterizes much of the debate. While few would become greatly agitated about the refusal of the Interstate Commerce Commission to permit an applicant to provide truck service between Peoria and East

St. Louis on grounds that it would impair the financial health of incumbent carriers, many can and do become highly agitated over a private enterprise's dumping chemical wastes into the Mississippi River. In the former case, the ICC may be guilty of parochialism and myopia, but in the latter the company is alleged to be engaged in a crime against society. And, while there is a remarkable degree of unity on the part of economists of all ideological persuasions over the appropriate solutions to problems of economic regulation (to wit, more competition and less regulation), there tends to be more diversity of views in the social area, often reflecting as much differences in ideology as in analysis.

In view of these characteristics, social regulation cries out for a "macro" approach rather than case-by-case reform. With economic regulation, potential excesses tend to be reined in by the industry that is the subject of regulation, with the result that too often the industry apparently "captures" the regulator. In the case of social regulation, the immediate objects of regulation—industrial firms—are often outorganized and outmaneuvered by the proponents of regulation, and thus the automatic restraint system tends to bog down. Moreover, few public officials, or even molders of public opinion, want to run the risk of being smitten with the scorn of social regulation's advocates or of being blamed for the tragedies that are bound to occur and that, arguably, could have been prevented by additional regulatory effort. In short, while no particular industry or firm is likely to initiate a wholesale confrontation with a particular regulatory agency, industry in general may well support an initiative to rein in the excesses of social regulators in general. And while few policy makers or policy molders are likely to take on any specific regulatory initiative, they might well be disposed toward some device to filter out the more egregious cases of regulatory excess.

Of the "macro" approaches addressed in recent years, nearly all have incorporated some requirement that agencies analyze the benefits and costs of their regulatory proposals. The Inflation Impact Statement program, initiated by President Ford in October of 1974, required agencies to analyze and consider the benefits and costs of alternative approaches. This requirement was carried over into Ford's successor Economic Impact Statement program and adopted by and large by President Carter in his Regulatory Analysis program. Various bills introduced in Congress would require the same thing, would extend the program to the so-called independent regulatory agencies, and would give the requirement the standing of law (rather than executive order).

At a conceptual level, few would disagree with cost-benefit analysis as a filter for agency decision making, for all it requires is that agencies engage only in activities that pass the test of common sense. The debate is over whether and how well this concept can be applied in practice. The costs of regulatory proposals are often difficult to measure, and arguably there are biases in the data on which such estimates are based. Benefits are even more difficult, especially in cases involving reduction in the risk of accidental injury or death. Beyond these problems are questions of redistribution. That is, it matters not only how much the benefits and costs are but who gets the benefits and who bears the costs.

The three presentations in this section illustrate and illuminate the problem of social regulation and the application of cost-benefit analysis. All three presenters are noted experts in the field and bring different perspectives to the issues.

The first presentation, by Dr. Suzanne Weaver, addresses primarily the reasons for the vehemence with which each side in the debate tends to express its own point of view and not only to discredit the opposition but to question its moral values.

The second presentation, by consumer advocate Mark Green, forcefully articulates the shortcomings of cost-benefit analysis as a final determinant of agency decision making. Mr. Green cites several examples of the difficulty of obtaining "objective" measures of benefits and reliable estimates of costs. He also raises significant ethical issues and warns policy makers and policy molders to be wary of the motives of those who advocate the application of cost-benefit analysis to social regulation.

The final presentation, by law professor Peter Schuck, espouses the need for cost-benefit analysis despite its methodological shortcomings. If we accept that all institutions, including regulation, are imperfect, the question becomes whether cost-benefit analysis, as a tool to be applied judiciously where appropriate, can improve regulatory performance. He answers in the affirmative, if only because the analysis would bring into the open many facts that regulators are prone to overlook.

None of these three presenters is ideologically wedded to the use of cost-benefit analysis, nor is any ideologically opposed. While Mr. Green would certainly circumscribe its application more than most, he still sees a role for it in regulatory decisions. While Ms. Weaver and Mr. Schuck advocate more use of the device than is currently practiced, neither would favor its rote application in all regulatory situations. Still, the differences in their perspectives and in the way they articulate their views illuminate the variety of issues involved in applying cost-benefit analysis to social regulation.

The Limits of
Cost-Benefit Analysis

Suzanne Weaver

Recently there was an exchange in the *Washington Post* between Mark Green of Congress Watch and Peter Schuck of the American Enterprise Institute on how much cost-benefit analysis could be reasonably used for the purpose of social regulation. I read through that exchange and, unsurprisingly for a representative of the *Wall Street Journal*, came to a somewhat different conclusion from Mr. Green's. Yet as I read his article, I was struck most of all by the extent to which I agreed with his analysis.

His argument, to quote from the *Post* article (January 21, 1979, section C1), is that "given the state of economic art, mathematical cost-benefit analyses are about as neutral as voter literacy tests in the Old South." That is not exactly a dispassionate way of putting it, but I think he is onto something. It may well be that by thinking explicitly about costs and benefits, even apart from the final verdict one reaches in a given case, one injects something into the debate that is not politically neutral and is, in some fundamental way, hostile to a large part of the current movement for social regulation.

This possibility came to me quite powerfully out of some work that I did recently, part of whose results appeared in the *Journal* as a feature article. The subject was the report produced a few years ago by Dr. Herbert Inhaber, a physicist working for the Atomic Energy Control Board of Canada. Inhaber made a first cut at going through the existing literature on the risks associated with various energy sources, in an attempt to figure out how the sources ranked.

The *Journal*'s involvement with the Inhaber report began some months ago when an article in the paper by another author mentioned the document in passing. After that mention, a strange thing happened. Our features editor, Thomas Bray, began to get detailed and passionate mail telling us what an egregiously bad piece of work the Inhaber report was. Some directed our attention to studies that, we were told, destroyed poor Inhaber quite completely. Mr. Bray—being, among other things, a first-rate journalist—thought that if Inhaber could make so many people so mad, he must have struck a nerve somewhere. I was asked to see what all the noise was about.

It turned out that Dr. Inhaber had backed into these attacks by attempting a variety of cost-benefit analysis. What he set out to do was to make a fairly straightforward calculation of various kinds of energy risks. He took all the literature on the various energy sources—conventional systems like coal, oil, and nuclear power, as well as the newer and more decentralized technologies like wind and solar energy—and added up the various risks to life and limb from each of them, all the way from the mining of the materials necessary to constructing each system, through the generation of power (including the backup facilities needed by decentralized systems), to final waste deposit. The resulting report was widely distributed, in no small part because Inhaber was the first person to do the unattractive but useful work of going through all the existing sources in the field and making the rather tedious calculations necessary to extract some kind of comparable data from them. But the report also got attention because it reached a rather startling conclusion. He said that the energy systems some people have touted as "clean," like solar energy and wind, could actually be riskier to society than some conventional systems, including nuclear power.

In retrospect, it is no great mystery why Inhaber's method of risk analysis would come up with such a conclusion. There are two kinds of structural reasons that contribute to the final verdict.

First, when one deals with a power source like nuclear energy, the maximum risks may be huge, but they are also remote. Any risk assessment method that counts both these factors will judge nuclear energy as relatively safe. Second, some of the new decentralized technologies are at the moment relatively inefficient and unreliable compared with the older systems. The low efficiency means that relatively large collectors are needed; large collectors take substantial amounts of material to build; and these materials pose risk to life and limb as they are mined, manufactured, and transported. Further, the low reliability of the new systems makes it necessary to take account of their backup systems and add the attendant risks of those into the total.

One can begin to see some of the structural problems with a method such as the one Inhaber used. Moreover, there are limitations from obvious and ordinary failings in the data—from the gaps, the ambiguities, and the errors in some of the studies, and the lies as well. It is also hardly likely that any researcher doing the first comprehensive collection job in this area can avoid contributing some plain ordinary mistakes of his own.

Besides those kinds of problems, there are middle-level conceptual problems that risk assessment of this sort is only beginning to deal with. For example, is it helpful to count up all the risks involved in huge solar collectors, if in fact the solar collectors will not be built until some way is found to bring the size and the cost down?

There are also the larger conceptual dilemmas. For instance, are there some possibilities connected with some kinds of energy production that are so horrible that it is quite reasonable to refuse to risk them now no matter how remote the chances of their occurrence? Or are there some kinds of dangers—for instance, the risk of producing a deformed child—that should be counted as being worse than illness or death or shortened life span?

As can readily be imagined, people wrote to Inhaber and the Atomic Energy Control Board with criticisms like this and, as a result, his report has been undergoing continual updating and correction. Yet none of these limitations explains the phenomenon that I was asked to investigate. The letters the *Wall Street Journal* was getting about the Inhaber report were not filled simply with criticism and suggestions for amendment. Instead, admitting to having no interest in amending the report, they thought it would be better if the document were obliterated altogether. They said the report deserved obliteration because it was so badly done but made no attempt to improve upon its analysis or come up with a fundamentally different conclusion.

The chief opponent of the Inhaber report has been John Holdren, a Berkeley physicist active in the movement against nuclear power and in promoting research into nonconventional energy sources. In their letters Dr. Holdren and his allies have, it is true, included specific criticisms of the report. They have argued that Inhaber overestimated material requirements for windmills, used conservative assumptions for some nonconventional energy sources that he did not apply to other systems, and misquoted sources on the various kinds of waste disposal risks in conventional energy. In addition to the specific criticisms, however, these various letters and publications have also assailed Inhaber with a most extraordinary kind of general invective. They have charged not only that he is in error but also that he is deliberately lying. They have called his document "by far the most imcompetent technical document . . . ever known to have been distributed by grown-ups." They have called it "garbage" and Inhaber a "buffoon." They have claimed flatly that any expert who defends the report either has not read it or is not an expert (which, in fact, is not true).

They have attempted, when talking to me by telephone, to make contact with my dim journalistic mind by explaining that they have used all these strong words because their situation is similar to that of the journalists who attacked Watergate. We had used very strong language,

I was told, to bring home the horror of the Watergate offense against society, and they were using strong language for the same reason to attack Inhaber.

Even for scientific controversies, this is a very strange and, of course, grossly indecent way to conduct a debate. For a while I confess I was mystified by the spectacle, but now I realize that Inhaber's critics were precisely right to be so upset. The offense of a document like this is not that it opts for one energy system over another. What is really going on is that it launches, in large part unintentionally, a much more dangerous kind of attack. A document like this operates on the assumption that the risks of the various energy sources may be different in degree but are not critically different in kind, if they were different in kind, one could not presume to compare them on any scale whatsoever.

To put it another way, the method of inquiry in the Inhaber report asserts by implication that energy sources are all somehow ethically equivalent and that they can, in the large, be judged according to the same standards. The enterprise suggests that a person who argues for one energy source over another cannot legitimately be judged a friend or enemy of the people simply by the choice he finally makes.

This kind of comparison takes a subject that has been spoken of in moral absolutes and presents it as something uncertain, ambiguous, subject to doubt and, perhaps, to compromise. Making an assertion like this—saying that an area of inquiry is subject to doubt—may seem a minimal thing. After all, it certainly does not guarantee what one's verdict will be in a particular case. One might follow a method like Inhaber's and then decide to ban nuclear power, or a suspected carcinogen, altogether. But Inhaber's kind of discourse is, in spite of such uncertainties, a significant threat to the strategy by which today's new regulation has been making its gains.

The argument surrounding much of the new regulatory movement is that technological capitalism is poisoning people. The corollary of the argument is that the poisons produced by this capitalism must be removed from the environment, that this is the only ethically responsible course for public policy to take, that those who raise cost considerations should not be trusted because their arguments are only smokescreens thrown up by the forces of greed.

For instance, Mark Green, in that *Washington Post* article, says that cost-benefit analysis might have prevented the Salk polio vaccine from coming on the market. He says it would have killed the idea of abolishing slavery. He says it would never have supported the child labor laws. He tells us that we cannot put a price on the child who may be saved from disfigurement from flammable sleepwear or on the worker who is saved from asbestos-induced cancer. The implication, which in its own way pollutes—indeed, poisons—the debate on regulation, is that those who talk in terms of cost-benefit analysis do not care about the child, do not care about the death.

I agree that these worries about children and lives are worries of the most profound kind. Yet I think the people who have been attacking cost-benefit analysis in this way have not expanded their field of moral worry far enough. For instance, on the matter of toxic chemicals, we are increasingly able to discover more not only about the toxic character of the workplace, which is serious enough, but also about the toxic character of natural processes. To take one example—and this is not a smokescreen, but a set of issues that at some point we must face in public policy—by now we are aware of huge numbers of carcinogens occurring naturally in the food supply, in foods ranging from fish to green vegetables. Does our growing knowledge of these things come without some obligation to act? And if we do have to act, how can we do so without some form of cost-benefit analysis, imperfect though it may be?

Mr. Green is right in calling attention to the fact that cost-benefit analysis is the enemy of the unbridled agenda of social regulation that he has been promoting. We will soon reach the time, however, when regulatory trade-offs in this area cannot be avoided. It might be good for public debate on the issue if more people began to point this out.

Cost-Benefit Analysis
as a Mirage

Mark J. Green

Murray Weidenbaum framed the issue best. He proposed that new regulations be limited to those things where total benefits to society exceed total costs. That is, the burden is on those who regulate to prove by more than one dollar or one life that the benefits exceed the cost. As a phrase, cost-benefit analysis deserves kudos. It ranks with truth-in-lending and pro-life as an apparently irrefutable slogan. Yet in practice it reminds me of a mirage in the desert—in reality it can turn to sand. This is because there are fundamental conceptual and empirical problems with the use of cost-benefit analysis.

First, we must recognize that regulated businesses always oppose the agency regulating them and, to a large extent, control the available cost data. Market economists should appreciate the bias whenever they use these data. For instance, in the late 1970s manufacturers of spray cans said banning fluorocarbons would destroy the industry. The automobile industry is claiming that requiring 27.5 fuel miles as opposed to 26.9 will destroy Western civilization. A community that has a vested interest and a prejudice will always exaggerate the cost of regulation.

One can say of this argument that it attacks the motives of a specific community. It does . . . and I think that is fair. Ms. Weaver has criticized it as ridiculous, as being based on analyses of greed. I think it is simply an analysis based on the record, on past cost studies. Hooker Chemical and Love Canal or Firestone and the Firestone 500 are examples: these companies had internal memoranda that indicated that they knew their product was unduly hazardous, but they continued to produce it. One has to be a true Dr. Pangloss to ignore the empirical record that undermines the credibility of cost studies coming out of the regulated community.

Second, benefits obviously can be quite real, although they may not surrender to an economist's yardstick. DES ingested by women today may cause cervical cancer two decades from now in their daughters, although we may not know how many. The Consumer Product Safety Commission estimated a substantial decrease in infant mortality because cribs no longer have the kinds of bars that strangle children.

113

It is hard to say how many or what the value of a baby's life is. Measurements of the valuation of life are often inconsistent. The National Highway Traffic Safety Administration estimates the cost at about $300,000, Robert Cotton at $1.5 million, and others at other figures.

The difficulty of valuation of benefits is particularly acute in social regulation. Economic regulation deals with rates and entry barriers, which are often reducible to economic equations and numbers. Hidden defects and externalities, the subjects of social regulation, are very difficult to translate into numbers. We know there is a value to being able to see across the city or the Grand Canyon, although it is difficult to put a dollar sign on it. Yet I must mention a benefit that strikes me as extraordinary and quite easily measured. It has been estimated that because one subsidiary of Allied Chemical put one insecticide, kepone, into the James River, it will now cost $8 billion to clean up that river. People often talk about the cost of regulation; this is a stunning example of the cost of *not* regulating.

A third problem with cost-benefit analysis is that cost studies to date not only have been one-sided and internal, but the studies of benefits have been one-sided and narrow in application. The 50,000 people, statistically, who will die next year from auto crashes are not lobbying for better benefit data. I would like to see NHTSA attempt to study the cost to members of a family of those killed in crashes in grief, loss of income, and so on. A victim study is needed to complement estimates of the cost to a company of installing bumper guards.

One of the forty-eight companies participating in the recent Business Roundtable study reported that it had spent a million dollars in cooperating with Arthur Andersen & Company to figure out indirect costs very precisely. Assuming the Business Roundtable study cost $40 million, that is the annual budget of the CPSC and 200 times the budget of Congress Watch.

Fourth, studies to date have had serious methodological deficiencies. Mr. Weidenbaum assumes the cost to the company in complying with passenger restraints is the same every year, although bumpers become lighter and stronger. There is interaction among market impurities that the studies in isolation do not show. Studies analyzing the effects of federal health and safety regulation define expenditures that reduce health costs as nonproductive investment because they do not produce wealth; this, I maintain, is an ideological conclusion prior to the fact.

Fifth, cost-benefit analysis of the strict mathematical kind assumes that economists and scientists can make calibrated judgments of the sort for which there are no tools at present. There have been ten studies of saccharin, for example, all documenting a relationship between the ingestion of saccharin and cancer, but one estimates that over the next fifty years there will be *0.5* deaths while the high one estimates *1.4 million* deaths. Risk assessment is very crude today. We can be confident that if an additive causes cancer in animals, it will cause cancer in human beings. But while one can demonstrate a correlation, it is impossible to document quantity.

Finally, in talking of problems, it is essential to note the current context. In the political context today, we cannot talk about Hamlet without the rotten state of Denmark. Similarly, we cannot talk about regulatory reform without acknowledging that, in my judgment, there is a substantial propaganda campaign being undertaken by companies unhappy with the imposition on them of any outside costs. They are against all regulation, good or bad. Mr. Breyer said no one is really against regulation per se. He should read the ads. My least favorite one is by Gould, Inc., which has a picture of the Statue of Liberty hung by a noose, the implication being "Strung up by Washington due to over-regulation."

As a final exercise, let us take cost-benefit analysis to its logical conclusion. Why not cost-benefit analysis of free speech, separation of church and state, protection of wildlife? In each of those instances, society has made a presumptive judgment that the policy is good—even though there may be obvious exceptions, like yelling "Fire" in a crowded theater. We do not engage in a case-by-case analysis of such policies because basic values are at stake; we cannot prove with numbers the benefit of free speech or separation of church and state. I would argue similarly that there should be a presumption in favor of expert agencies appointed and confirmed by the president and Congress that, after hearing all evidence in due process hearings, arrive at a judgment. This judgment, also, is surely subject to checks and oversight: first, there is the process producing the legislative bill, second, due process procedures before the agency; third, inevitable court appeals by unhappy businesses; and fourth, the legislative effort to overrule it.

This is not to be anti-intellectual. Obviously, someone has to make the judgment and the trade-offs. The 55-miles-per-hour speed limit is not a perfect judgment. It could be 50 or 30 or 70. It is a trade-off of lives against convenience. That is done on the basis of the evidence brought before the regulatory agency and the judgment of the agency; it is not based on any formalistic, precise computation, which cannot now be made. Before regulators make a decision, they have before them the best estimate of a proposed rule's adverse consequences, if any, to the company and to consumers generally, as well as the best estimate of its economic and noneconomic benefits. They do not have a precise, numerical cost-benefit calculation. In this view I am joined not only by Congressman John Moss and the report that I cited but by the Senate Governmental Affairs Committee and the General Accounting Office. *Business Week*, also my ally, has said that economists cannot agree on cost-benefit formulas because the "benefits" are so hard to calculate. In testimony two weeks ago, the chairman of the Chamber of Commerce said, "Of course, we are not talking about strict cost-benefit study, because you can't measure benefits." Cost-benefit analysis should be used not as a straitjacket but as a tool to aid regulation, subject to review by the political and judicial processes.

A Tool for
Assessing Social Legislation

Peter H. Schuck

My perspective on cost-benefit analysis is straightforward and simple, reflecting my own experience in government. It begins with the premise that many of the public policy issues that regulators face are extremely complex, not technically but as matters of judgment. They are questions of allocation of scarce resources among competing social ends. In many respects they resemble what Guido T. Calabresi has referred to as "tragic choices": they require us to sacrifice some things to achieve others. Very rarely are the issues that a regulator confronts simply ones of health and safety, on the one hand, versus profits and dollars on the other. That kind of formulation ignores the fundamental characteristics of the regulatory process and of the most significant regulatory questions. I would like to discuss three of those fundamental characteristics.

The first is the overwhelming uncertainty that attends regulatory decisions. There are uncertainties regarding the causal relationships and the presumed benefits that underlie regulatory decisions. In the area of chemical carcinogens, for example, there is tremendous uncertainty regarding dose-response relationships. Even where the causal relationship is established, we do not know what the threshold of danger is, or if indeed there is a threshold. We do not know very much about what substitutes will be used for chemicals that we are either banning or regulating. There is some evidence that in many cases the substitute chemical has been more damaging.

On the cost side, regulation often affects competition and industry structure. We have little information about the effects of regulation on technological change and industrial innovation. We also do not know very much about the ways consumers and industry will respond to a regulatory decision. The substantial uncertainties on both the benefit and cost sides are pertinent to the question of what tools the regulatory decision maker should employ.

A second characteristic of the regulatory process, which would exist even if this uncertainty were somehow dispelled, is that the decision invariably involves trading off one good thing against another. For example, there is often a trade-off between the health of one group and

117

the health of another. We are concerned not only about the health of people who live near the nuclear power plant at Three Mile Island but also about the health of the group that will mine the substitute for nuclear fuel, that is, coal, and about the health of people living near coal-fired plants who are subject to their pollutants. The choice is health versus health. Similarly, there is often a trade-off between the jobs and prosperity of one group, such as those industries protected by import restrictions, and the jobs and prosperity of another group, such as those industries that would benefit from free trade. Another common trade-off is that between the health of one group, such as consumers, and the jobs and prosperity of another group, such as workers in a particularly dangerous industry. Further, we often face a trade-off between the health of a group, such as cotton textile workers threatened with byssinosis, and the jobs and prosperity of that same group, which are threatened by the economic dislocations resulting from particular regulatory restrictions designed to protect their health.

These unpleasant realities are not unique to the capitalist system; they will attend any modern economic system. They are simply realities of life that we must face and do our best to deal with. It is important to contradict the notion that we are dealing with clear moral decisions in most of the trade-offs we confront. While they clearly do have moral elements, they are fundamentally choices between competing and often compelling moral claims.

A third element of regulatory decisions that pertains to the use of cost-benefit analysis is the tremendous disparity in the intensity of preference of the various people and groups who are affected by a regulation. For some interests, a particular regulation might literally be a matter of life and death—for example, workers employed in very dangerous industries, workers whose jobs are eliminated by regulation, communities whose basic industry, such as strip mining, is affected by regulation. Other interests, such as consumers benefited by a product safety regulation, may not even be aware that the regulation exists or that their particular interest is being invoked. They may not care one way or the other about the value being asserted in support of that regulation or may not feel that the achievement of that value is worth whatever it costs.

Each of these characteristics—uncertainty, the necessity of trade-offs, and the great disparity in intensity of preferences among affected groups—is exacerbated in the case of social regulation. Here I want to confront an argument that has been made by Mr. Green and others, the argument that while cost-benefit analysis may be important in economic or cartel regulation, it is somehow inappropriate in the case of social regulation. I maintain that each of the three elements that I have discussed is, in fact, more troublesome in social regulation and that cost-benefit analysis is at least as justified in the one area as in the other.

The area of social regulation involves relatively great uncertainties because we so seldom possess reliable data on the health, safety, and other effects of either the status quo or proposed regulations. In addition, social regulation, in contrast to economic regulation, entails a vast increase in the number of industries and activities being regulated. For example, the Occupational Safety and Health Administration regulates 5 million workplaces in thousands of different industries. Compare the regulatory task involved in arriving at sensible decisions on a standard to impose in a context like that with the task of the Civil Aeronautics Board in regulating the airline industry's prices and terms of service. As difficult as the CAB's task may be, it is child's play compared with the complexity and uncertainty that face the regulator at OSHA.

Second, trade-offs are demonstrably more difficult in the area of social regulation because they involve objectives that society values so very highly—health, safety, and human life. The costs of social regulation are highly visible, concentrated as they are in particular firms, particular workers, and even particular consumers, that is, the consumers of the regulated product. In comparison, the Interstate Commerce Commission's cartel regulation involves relatively mundane, though certainly important, social and economic values. There the costs of regulation are not visible to the consumer, nor are they concentrated on particular industries.

Finally, the disparity of intensity of preference is considerably exacerbated in social regulation because the number of people affected and the diversity of their interests are so much greater than in the case of a regulatory system applicable to only one industry.

I draw several implications from all this. The first is that social regulators need all the help they can get in making these very difficult judgments, these tragic choices. Cost-benefit analysis, even recognizing all its very substantial imperfections, can provide that help. No knowledgeable defender of such analysis would argue that it should be anything more than a tool to inform choice. Anybody who suggests that it should be plugged in mechanically to generate a result that a decision maker must accept is either misinformed or a fool.

It is striking to me that the same people who are willing to man the barricades to defend the National Environmental Policy Act and environmental impact statements are equally passionate in their hostility to cost-benefit analysis. It is a source of wonder because in this view the fundamental principles of ecology—that the physical world is complex, that everything in it is related to everything else, and that we should not tromp into that world with three-league boots until we know what we are doing—suddenly become inapplicable when we enter the social world. Surely the social world is no less complex or less susceptible to analysis than the physical world. There must be some other reason for treating the two situations differently. I have my suspicions about what the reason is. In any event, this attitude conceals a profound inconsistency.

It defies understanding why anyone who is faced with the kinds of decisions that I have described would want to be denied the assistance of a competent cost-benefit analysis. That kind of analysis does not and should not determine the decision. What it can do is illuminate the implications of the choices facing the regulator. From my experience, cost-benefit analyses help in many cases to improve the decision ultimately made by government.

The second major conclusion that I draw is implicit in all this. Cost-benefit analysis is at least as appropriate or necessary—indeed, I would argue more necessary—to social regulation as to economic regulation. We do not really need a cost-benefit analysis to tell us that when the ICC restricts entry, it is going to have adverse effects on consumers. We do need some kind of analysis where the decision involves the kinds of uncertainties, consequences, and ramifications in the complex social environment that are entailed in many health and safety regulations.

The third implication is that significant regulatory decisions are ineluctably political, in two important senses. First, as I have observed, they require numerous judgments about trade-offs of competing social values. Second, and perhaps less recognizable by opponents of cost-benefit analysis, intensity of preferences ought to receive recognition and weight in the decision-making process. It is a shallow view of democracy that accords as much weight to my convenience as a consumer as it does to your livelihood as a worker. The political process is supposed to weigh those differential impacts and take them into account, not treat them as having equal significance. Cost-benefit analysis, while it cannot make those judgments, can at least illuminate the choices.

Regulatory agencies are, and in my view ought to be, part of the far larger system of political institutions and forces. Just as we expect the courts to attend to what legislatures and executive agencies are doing, so regulatory agencies—at least in the nonadjudicatory, essentially legislative functions that constitute the bulk of their important decisions—should be exposed to, rather than immunized from, those institutions and forces. The legal rules that govern these relationships and influences should be designed not to eliminate them but rather to make them sufficiently visible that politicians can be held accountable for them. Our objective should be to make regulators and those officials who seek to influence them politically accountable for their inevitably political decisions, rather than pretend that they are making merely technical decisions that should be "purified" of political influence. I believe that much of the criticism of cost-benefit analysis reflects a denial of the fundamental notion that what regulatory decision makers inevitably do is to make decisions that are ultimately political in the fullest sense of the term. Rather than transform that necessity into a virtue, these critics fall back on an illusionary view of the decision-making process as essentially technical. This enables them to sidestep the most serious need of our system—to require regulators to be made accountable for their decision.

Finally, the imperfections and limitations of cost-benefit analysis should be squarely addressed and acknowledged. There is no reason to apologize for them. They are inherent in the limitations of human rationality. Some improvements can be made in cost-benefit analysis, but many shortcomings will inevitably remain, and there will always be incentives to distort and misuse this kind of analysis. I know no regulators who are not well aware of all these imperfections; nor do I know any regulators who view cost-benefit analysis as anything more than a sometimes useful, but almost never decisive, tool.

The real question is not whether cost-benefit analysis can be misused—any tool can be misused—but rather whether it will be used to its full potential. One part of this issue is whether the political process permits and encourages diverse interests to argue about the premises, the values, the calculations, and other elements of the analysis in a way that fleshes out the issues for the regulator. I believe that on the whole it does. Indeed, it is very difficult for me to take seriously the critique of those opposed to cost-benefit analysis when I observe the behavior of OSHA, EPA, and other social regulators that clearly are quite sensitive to consumer and environmental interests and when I observe the considerable extent to which environmental and other "public interests" are represented in the process. If we as a society conclude that those interests are not sufficiently well represented, there are a number of ways in which that problem could be remedied. I have spent much of my career supporting such efforts, and there is no reason to believe that the process has yet achieved perfection.

Whether the process has considered all relevant interests is a very different question, I maintain, from whether a particular point of view will ultimately prevail. We cannot infer from the fact that Congress Watch, or the Environmental Defense Fund, or the Business Roundtable did not get their way on a particular regulation that their interests were not adequately and fairly represented or that cost-benefit analysis was misused by the decision maker.

121

The second question regarding potential use is this: if the regulators are not to use this kind of analysis, or something very much like it, to pose the fundamental questions that they must answer, what criteria *should* they use? Should they use the presence or absence of an economic interest animating the proponents or opponents of the proposed regulation? That is not a very satisfactory criterion of choice; yet it is the one that many critics of cost-benefit analysis implicitly offer in its stead. The road to hell, it has been said, is paved with good intentions. Something more is needed. I certainly do not claim that cost-benefit analysis will ever answer the most difficult questions that confront regulators, but it can contribute to better decisions and deliberations in the political process by increasing the probability that the regulatory decision will consider and reflect the full range of interests affected by regulation in our society.

Summary of Discussion

In the discussion that followed the presentations on cost-benefit analysis, two questions came up. In response to Mr. Schuck's observation that most regulatory decisions are political, one participant asked how these decisions could be forced back into the political arena. Mr. Schuck suggested that the committees in Congress that oversee the agencies and authorize their budgets take greater pains to enunciate the principles that agencies should follow in making their decisions. He also recommended that instead of questioning intervention by the White House in regulatory decision making in the executive branch, regulatory observers should encourage it to do so, especially in cases involving informal rule making, *provided* such intervention is made a part of the public record.

Another member of the audience suggested to Mr. Green that the appropriate role of government is to disseminate information on hazards but that the choice to work or live in hazardous areas or to purchase unsafe products should be left to individuals. Mr. Green responded that the decisions of individuals often have effects on others as well as themselves. It might seem reasonable to give the owner of an automobile the option of having it equipped with safety devices, but a passenger would not have the same option. He argued also that in many cases, disseminating the requisite information is just not feasible. Many purchases are quite complicated—life insurance and certain consumer products are examples. Moreover, he said, in some cases any reasonable estimate of regulatory benefits so overwhelms costs that it makes eminent sense for collective action to overrule individual decisions.

Part
Seven

The Administration's Regulatory
Reform Initiatives

Introduction

Timothy B. Clark, Chairman

I suspect that the concern about overregulation needs to be understood by raising two points. One is that poll after poll has shown that the public does not want to back away from the environmental, health, and safety goals of the regulatory statutes. There is no desire in the public's mind . . . to downplay our decisions to clean up the water, the air, and the environment and to bring safety to the workplace. There does, however, seem to be a public perception that the way we have gone about accomplishing those goals is neither concise nor clear. Regulatory programs are filled with duplication, overlaps, and all those classic cases of mismanagement.

A major reason for that interpretation is that when we enacted those laws, we knew what we wanted to do before we knew how to do it.

These remarks of Mr. Granquist reflect the Carter administration's frustration as it attempts to deal with the divergent patterns of public opinion concerning regulation. The administration has attempted in various ways to bring a semblance of rationality to the regulatory morass it inherited and to exert some control over the agencies, at least those in the executive branch. Still, Mr. Rogers reminds us that the laws and the ensuing regulations are needed.

The president's moves to deregulate industries long controlled by the government for economic reasons, such as airlines and trucking, are but a small part of the administration's efforts. The focus here is the burdens imposed on the economy by agencies whose missions are more social than economic—the Environmental Protection Agency, the Occupational Safety and Health Administration, the Consumer Product Safety Commission, and others—and the efforts under way to reform that aspect of regulation.

The Regulatory Council, chaired by Mr. Costle, was established in October 1978 with thirty-five member agencies and the mission of better coordinating their regulatory endeavors. (Mr. Costle's own agency, the EPA, is working to introduce economic incentives and other reforms in its programs.) The Regulatory Analysis Review Group, chaired by the Council of Economic Advisers and described here by Mr. Eads, is an interagency group established in early 1978 to review each year ten to twenty major regulations proposed by the agencies and attempt to force them to meet their goals as efficiently as possible.

Through a presidential executive order, the administration is attempting to impose a more disciplined thought process on the agencies. Requirements for more rigorous analysis of the economic consequences of proposed regulations, opportunity for earlier public review, and sunset reviews of existing rules are among the features of this effort, as Mr. Granquist describes. The administration also believes that it is important to enact legislation making Congress a partner in the program and extending its requirements to such independent regulatory agencies as the Federal Communications Commission and the Interstate Commerce Commission.

The complexity of regulating the economy is becoming increasingly apparent, Mr. Eads argues, especially to those charged with actually doing the regulating. In the next two years, the government will be "developing sufficient understanding of this complexity to enable us to define the organizational and legal changes that will be necessary if we are to manage the regulatory process effectively and to enable us to understand the trade-offs required, the limits of analysis, and the abilities of organizations."

Critics of regulation point the finger of blame at Congress for writing laws that are either too vague or too specific but whose costs to the private sector Congress never recognizes. A principal author of many of the most important of these laws, including the Clean Air Act and the Safe Drinking Water Act, was Mr. Rogers. As a member of the House from Florida for twenty-four years before retiring in 1979, Mr Rogers chaired the Subcommittee on Health and the Environment of the House Committee on Interstate and Foreign Commerce.

Mr. Rogers defends Congress's impulse to save the environment, promote public health, ensure workers' safety, and protect consumers. At the same time, he recognizes that the regulatory "pendulum" may have swung too far to the left and that it is time to bring it back to the center, where costs and benefits could balance. Yet the administration's creation of new institutions to oversee the regulatory process may simply compound the problems, according to Mr. Rogers. He raises the specter of "institutional polarization within the executive branch" as a consequence of the new institutions. He also attacks the "false precision" of the regulatory cost-benefit analysis advocated by the administration. What is needed, in Mr. Rogers's view, is a proper balance, trying to ward off the excess but still do something about the needs.

Mr. Crandall strikes a gloomy note by challenging the idea that there are *any* significant benefits from regulation. The administration's proposals to deregulate surface transportation would correct a mistake of nearly a hundred years' standing—starting when the Interstate Commerce Commission was created in 1887—and more recent legislative errors might take as long to correct, says Mr. Crandall. Mr. Crandall agrees with the earlier diagnosis of the problem—"that we knew what we wanted to do before we knew how to do it." In so saying, Mr. Granquist effectively set the tone for the debate on the administration's initiatives for regulatory reform.

The Environmental Protection Agency's Initiatives

Douglas M. Costle

The three things I would like to address are the Environmental Protection Agency's response to the president's drive to improve the efficiency of regulation, our efforts in the area of cost-benefit analysis of regulation, and the work of the Regulatory Council that I chair.

The EPA's initiatives in regulatory reform include approximately thirty-four different projects. I will describe a few that suggest the general character of our reform efforts.

First, we have begun a review of all existing regulations to determine which can be eliminated, simplified, replaced with alternatives, or otherwise improved. Fortunately, the most recent statutes underlying EPA's activities—especially the 1977 Clean Air and Water Acts—provide an impetus for sunset review of regulations. Until recently there was no self-executing pressure on the federal government to review what it had already done, to ask critically whether a job is getting done and whether it is being done efficiently or effectively. Having a few of our governing statutes amended to provide for such review adds work initially, to be sure, but we have already seen that it can make a positive difference.

Last July, for example, we revised the water pollution guidelines for thirteen industries whose discharges are not toxic. Primary among them was the food-processing industry. We estimated that these changes will save about $200 million a year for the affected industries out of a total bill of $500 million, and this with no sacrifice in water quality benefits at all. This is evidence that we are getting better at analyzing sensibly the regulatory situations in which we find ourselves.

As part of a congressionally mandated review of air quality standards, we reviewed the health effects of photochemical oxidants and, as a result, recalibrated that standard. By law the basis for the revision was an assessment of health effects alone, but we think that it will also result in a cost reduction of as much as $1 billion a year over the former standard while at the same time protecting the air quality–related health benefits that the Congress had in mind when it passed the Clean Air Act.

In addition, we are exploring a new approach to controlling air and water emissions from industrial facilities. Where possible, instead of telling plant managers how low emissions must be from each pipe within a plant, we are trying, where it makes sense to do so, to regard the plant as a single pollutant generator and to give the managers flexibility to find the cheapest way of limiting emissions, as long as the total from all pipes does not exceed current standards. Because of the notion of a big bubble over an entire plant, which is then viewed as a single source of a specific pollutant, this concept is known as the bubble approach. A key to it, of course, is that we are trying to control like pollutants.

Finally, we have joined with several other regulatory agencies, particularly in the health and safety area—the Food and Drug Administration, the Occupational Safety and Health Administration, the Consumer Product Safety Commission, and, since January, the Food Safety and Quality Service of the Department of Agriculture—in developing uniform approaches to regulatory matters that concern two or more of us. We discovered, for example, that we all had a regulatory interest in and were impelled by our respective statutes to deal with a variety of toxic chemical substances. Indeed, we found twenty-four such substances in which two or more of us were contemplating action. Having discovered that, we are now preparing coordinated plans.

We are also developing an approach to a national carcinogen regulatory policy. This is distinct from a national cancer policy, which would require us to consider research investment as well. This policy addresses the basic question of how to regulate carcinogens in a human environment. It involves us in four subquestions, two of which are scientific and have been the subject of considerable debate. First, how do we recognize a carcinogen? Second, how do we assess the likely health impact of that substance? The five agencies I have just mentioned recently published a risk assessment document that attempts to pull together the current best thinking of the government as well as of private university scientists on those two critical issues.

The other two questions are policy questions, and they are more difficult. First, having decided that certain substances are carcinogenic and having assessed their probable risk to human health, how do we set priorities? Which substances should we go after first, and why? We have to develop criteria by which to make those judgments, because it is clear that we cannot be everywhere and do everything at once. Finally, our most difficult question is how to regulate the carcinogens. We have a spectrum of legislated approaches. Indeed, the Congress, by virtue of originating legislation from a variety of committees and subcommittees, has in effect enacted a portfolio approach to the question of regulating carcinogens. This is not, I might add, an entirely irrational approach. In fact, we are discovering that some of the judgments Congress has made about regulating carcinogens are very reasonable. I hope that by midsummer we will have a good first cut at a national carcinogen policy and that it will involve all the agencies engaged in regulating carcinogens.

Traditionally, EPA regulations have been of the command-and-control variety. That is, we tell industries and municipalities what they must do and when; in the case of failure or refusal, we enforce those requirements with certain mandatory steps. But we have found that litigation often benefits the polluter more than it does the public. By dragging a suit through the courts as long as possible, a polluter can postpone necessary capital expenditure and delay using pollution controls long enough to gain a substantial financial advantage over its complying competitors. That is why our regulatory reform effort is also aimed at seeking alternatives to the usual command-and-control mechanisms. In particular, we are looking for ways to join pollution control and economic incentives.

Many of the ideas we are discussing have not yet been fully developed or tested. I feel strongly, however, that we should be experimenting, trying new approaches, new ideas, and new concepts so that as the laws evolve—and they will evolve—we can incorporate hard experience instead of just theory into regulatory reform.

Among the new approaches is offset banking. This is a system that permits industries and municipalities to reduce pollution more than the required amount and to consider a portion of that reduction a sort of credit. The credit can be used for future expansion of facilities, or it can be traded or sold to another facility in the area. The system permits economic growth to continue in a dirty air area as long as progress toward attainment of the national ambient air quality standards continues as well. We are also exploring the possibility of controlling the production and the use of chlorofluorocarbons—other than those from aerosol sprays, which have now been banned—through marketable permits. Permits for environmentally acceptable amounts of chlorofluorocarbons might be auctioned off to the highest bidder. In addition, to eliminate the benefits of court delays, we are evaluating systems of economic penalties equal to the amounts polluters save through violations of standards or through poor operation or maintenance of pollution control equipment.

One of the most challenging aspects of regulatory reform is improving our ability to do analysis, particularly to do meaningful cost-benefit analysis. Costs are relatively easy to assess; benefits are not. Invariably, benefits involve human health, and it is extremely hard to put a dollar value on that. It is also difficult to put a quantitative value on the probabilities about which scientists themselves disagree. The state of the art is not advanced, but the effort is well worth pursuing.

Our Economic Analysis Division, for example, is directing a two-year study of six major EPA decisions in order to develop a series of prototype analyses. The study will draw on benefit estimation methods developed for an EPA study of air pollution control benefits and additional studies by the National Academy of Sciences on the possible costs and benefits of controlling twelve pollutants.

Finally, the Regulatory Council deserves some mention. It was established by the president in November 1978 and now includes thirty-five departments and agencies as members. We have already published the first edition of the Regulatory Calendar, which lists the most significant regulatory actions now being considered throughout the government. Subsequent editions will be published every six months.

The calendar is much more than a simple list. It is the first significant tool we in government have had, crude though it is, to assess the overall direction of regulation and to spot sectors that face multiple regulatory actions at the same time. There are sectors where duplicate and sometimes inconsistent regulations have an extraordinary impact. The Maryland State Medical Association, for example, recently identified 40 federal and 60 state entities that regulate hospitals. A 1978 study by the Hospital Association of New York State identified 140 regulatory agencies and estimated that regulation may add as much as $38 per patient per day in New York. Such costs may be outweighed by corresponding benefits, but, again, they may not. We need a mechanism to examine that question systematically.

The Regulatory Council plans to examine the impact of multiple regulation on a number of industries. Although the final choices have not been made, the leading candidates for such analysis include housing, financial institutions, steel, primary metals, and the auto industry.

This administration is committed to making federal regulation as cost-effective as possible. At the same time, I want to stress that the administration does not intend to achieve cost savings at the expense of legitimate public health commitments. As deregulation of the airline industry suggests, some federal restrictions have outlived their effectiveness. In the areas of health and safety, however, I believe our analysis will show that the most important question is not whether to regulate but how to do so most effectively.

Reform through the
Regulatory Analysis Review Group

George C. Eads

As a new arrival at the Council of Economic Advisers, not yet confirmed, I am not in a position to review the history of its activities in the regulatory area. I can, however, describe what we are doing now and what I believe we should be doing in the future.

The CEA has been involved in the traditional regulatory areas for a long time. In telecommunications and transportation, for example, we have long argued that regulation should be reduced or eliminated wherever possible. We were among the first advocates of airline deregulation, and our interest in trucking deregulation extends back almost ten years. We expect to continue to fight for reduced regulation in these areas. In addition, the CEA will maintain its generally procompetitive stance toward government policy overall, including agricultural policy, although it is no secret we have not always been successful. In the debate over national health insurance, we are supporting policies to encourage competition insofar as feasible. In trade, we continue as best we can to fight protectionism and to get the cost of protectionist measures made explicit.

I recognize, however, that the greatest interest in this forum is in our work in "social" regulation. We are in the forefront of the effort to see that regulatory actions of the government give due allowance to the impact they have on the economy. We do this in several ways. One major way is through our participation in the Regulatory Analysis Review Group. Executive Order 12044 requires that major rules and regulations be accompanied by a regulatory analysis that contains an explicit statement of alternatives and that is made available in the public comment process early enough to matter. I am quite impressed with the advance this new process represents. When a regulatory analysis appears on a major rule or regulation, the RARG has to decide whether to undertake a review of it. Our resources limit the number of regulations we can review to between ten and twenty per year. Because we have also agreed not to concentrate too heavily on one agency, we have a "rule of four"—no one agency will be subjected to more than four reviews in a calendar year.

134

This first decision—whether to subject a new regulatory analysis to review—is made by the Executive Committee of the RARG. That consists of members from the CEA, the Office of Management and Budget, and two others who rotate every six months. Currently, those two members represent the Department of Commerce and the Department of Health and Human Services. When a regulatory analysis is considered for review, the agency that prepared it appears, and there is a general discussion about whether a review is appropriate and what it could contribute.

If the decision is made to review the regulation, a statement of the issues that will be addressed is sent to the agency together with the notice of review. We announce our intention to make a filing, and this statement is placed in the public record. The filing is drafted by staff of the CEA or the Council on Wage and Price Stability and circulated to all members of the RARG for comment. We then hold a meeting in which comments are received and incorporated, but if the results do not meet with everyone's satisfaction, there is a provision for filing dissents. At the close of the comment period, the document is filed as part of the public record as representing a statement of administration views on the issues raised.

One thing that I was concerned about when I arrived at the CEA was that there was no way for the agencies, the public, or even the member groups' staffs to know in advance the activities in which RARG might have an interest. A notice of proposed rule making would appear in the *Federal Register* and, if it was major, we would look at the regulatory analysis and make a decision. In effect, we were operating in a reactive mode.

Recently, with the publication of the Regulatory Calendar, it became possible for us to provide some advance notice of the regulations we might be reviewing. I asked the staff of the Council on Wage and Price Stability to prepare a list of what appeared to be the most important forthcoming rule makings over the remainder of calendar 1979. This was drawn primarily from the Regulatory Calendar, but we supplemented it where necessary through contacts with individual agencies, to confirm both that the regulation was indeed likely to come out during the calendar year and that it did appear to be major. I circulated this list to all members of the RARG and asked the Regulatory Council to circulate it to all its members; it has now been released to the public. The list gives a general notion about our possible review candidates. There is no guarantee that all the items on the list will actually be reviewed by RARG—we probably will not have the resources to do that, and in any case, we will still decide on a case-by-case basis as each regulation comes out. Inclusion on the list does, however, create a strong presumption that when one of these regulations is actually proposed, a review may be warranted.

What priorities should the RARG use in choosing items to review? The notion that a very small group of people can or should act as a watchdog for the executive branch regulatory agencies is a little overblown. We certainly cannot do this, even if we limit ourselves to the most important regulations. What I would like to see the RARG evolve into is an organization that raises questions that individual agencies either cannot or will not ask as they go about doing their analyses.

There is also a growing recognition that in a number of cases more than one agency is concerned with the outcome of rule making. I commend Mr. Costle for his leadership in getting the agencies together on certain of these regulations. There is not enough of that done within the government. One of the things I think RARG can do is to draw attention to cases where a particular regulation not only has important costs or benefits itself but also has a major impact on something another agency is doing.

The process of managing the regulatory process is extremely important. We are entering a period when the complexity of regulating the economy is becoming increasingly apparent to all, especially those charged with actually doing the regulating. I see the next few years as a period of developing sufficient understanding of this complexity to enable us to define the organizational and legal changes that will be necessary if we are to manage the regulatory process effectively and to enable us to understand the trade-offs required, the limits of analysis, and the abilities of organizations. This will be one of the major issues that this—or any—administration will face over the next decade: how and to what extent can one effectively manage the regulatory process we have created over the past decade? It will be a major challenge, and I look forward to being a part of it.

The Role of the Office of Management and Budget

Wayne G. Granquist

A proposal is now before Congress to make into law some aspects of the president's Executive Order 12044. I would like to describe this proposed legislation and then to give a personal assessment of where we stand in regulatory reform—our view of the cause of the problem and of what we think we can do about it.

I suspect it is appropriate to put our activities at the Office of Management and Budget in historical perspective. That perspective is quite a simple one.

OMB's purpose in the regulatory area is twofold. It is, first, to discontinue those schemes, like airline regulation, that we believe have outlived their usefulness. Second, it is to pursue the statutory goals set forth in the environmental, safety, and health areas and to manage the flood of regulations resulting from the scores of programs set up from 1969 through 1975 in a way that accomplishes those goals in the most constructive and the least burdensome acceptable manner.

In proposing the regulation reform legislation, we address the second point. The bill now before Congress carries on the philosophy underlying the executive order—strict accountability on the part of agency heads to achieve the goals of their statutory programs in ways that are the least burdensome, consistent with the law.

The bill, like the executive order, provides some tools to help administrators accomplish that result. The first and perhaps most important tool is what we call regulatory analysis. Regulatory analysis has an element of cost-benefit analysis in it, but we recognize that the state of the art in that area is far from perfect. So, rather than cost-benefit analysis, we prefer to call it a rigorous analysis of options that should commence at the beginning or as close to the beginning of the rule-making process as possible. Then the agency head and the public can evaluate various alternative ways to accomplish those goals. Before the executive order, we had found that economic impact statements were too often manufactured at the end of the rule-making process as a justification for a decision already made. We are trying to make the development of alternatives occur much earlier in the process. That is

137

why, for example, we require that draft regulatory analyses be published at the time of the notice of proposed rule making for public reaction. We hope that the public will look at and comment on the alternatives.

We are concerned about public participation, and we believe that better and broader participation produces better rules. We have therefore increased the time of the public participation from the customary thirty days to sixty under the executive order. That provision is carried over into the new legislation we have proposed to Congress. The legislation also provides for annual funding of $14 million for participation by consumer groups and other interest groups that would not otherwise be represented in rule-making proceedings and that could play a significant role in those proceedings.

Third, we require in the executive order and have proposed in the legislation a periodic review, over a ten-year cycle, of the major regulations of each agency to ensure that the public and the agency head examine their workability and determine whether they are still necessary.

The bill also addresses the formal rule-making process: it would amend the Administrative Procedure Act to require much more expedited procedures than are currently in effect. Our effort here is to emphasize informal and written communications while getting away from the interminable cross-examination that has come to characterize formal rule making.

Finally, the bill would change the personnel system for administrative law judges, from one that is, in essence, a lifetime tenure with Civil Service status to one in which there are fixed terms of seven years. Judges' terms might be renewed or not renewed by the chairman of the Administrative Conference upon examination of their performance.

Since many of these requirements are now covered by the executive order, the question is often asked why we think we need congressional action. There are two reasons. One, we believe it is important for Congress to ratify our judgment that we must manage the regulatory process better—that managing the process is as critical to success as the original legislative process of setting out regulatory goals. Second, we made a conscious decision at the time of the executive order to ask the independent regulatory commissions to comply voluntarily, but we did not attempt to seek jurisdiction over them. The legislation would apply the requirements of the executive order to these agencies. These rigorous management processes and procedures must, in our opinion, be applied to the entire rule-making component of the government, not only to the executive branch.

What are the limits of our legislation? It does not apply to or amend underlying regulatory statutes such as the Clean Air Act or the Clean

Water Act. For that reason, we endorse strongly—with Senator Edmund Muskie and others—sunset review legislation. We believe it necessary to look at the underlying programs regularly. The Clean Water Act and the Clean Air Act already have sunset provisions in them; other agencies and other legislation do not. We hope the House will act on this important concept this year as the Senate did last year.

Who is to blame for overregulation? First, we ought to consider what we mean by overregulation. In my experience at OMB, I have discovered that regulation has about as many meanings as there are audiences. I suspect that the concern about overregulation needs to be understood by raising two points. One is that poll after poll has shown that the public does not want to back away from the environmental, health, and safety goals of the regulatory statutes. There is no desire in the public's mind, at least as far as I can see, to downplay our decisions to clean up the water, the air, and the environment and to bring safety to the workplace. There does, however, seem to be a public perception that the way we have gone about accomplishing those goals is neither concise nor clear. Regulatory programs are filled with duplication, overlaps, and all those classic examples of mismanagement.

A major reason for that interpretation is that when we enacted those laws, we knew what we wanted to do before we knew how to do it. Moreover, Congress, beginning in the 1960s and extending into the early 1970s, was an activist body whose constituents were crying out for it to do something about things that they increasingly perceived as real dangers in our highly technological society. Congress acted in its wisdom, but without what I would call a central place to stand. There was no guiding vision of what these regulatory schemes would accomplish, of what they would cost, or of how their impact on various sectors or various industries would be measured. Our response, therefore, has been to fill the vacuum—to create some of the regulatory-process tools that were absent initially. That is the goal we will continue to pursue.

Alternatives to the Administration's Initiatives

Robert W. Crandall

Much of what we hear about regulatory reform does not really address what most of us, at least among economists, think are the basic problems of regulation. An economist in government—and I once struggled with the role Mr. Eads now finds himself in—quickly comes to realize that there are limits to what we can accomplish by doing more analysis, forcing analysis on agencies, trying to bring the pressure of the executive office of the president to bear on the regulators. The problem is that one very soon encounters someone, a member of the bar who has been appointed to a job as assistant administrator somewhere, who says that the idea one is proposing makes a lot of sense but it cannot be done because of the law. The *law* tells you that you cannot do what makes sense. As a result, if we are to improve the regulatory process, we have to make some changes in the enabling legislation for the various regulatory agencies.

Problems with the law go back a very long time and have played a large role in the history of regulation. The first of the major federal regulatory statutes was the Act to Regulate Commerce in 1887. At that time there was considerable sentiment even among the financial barons of Wall Street that regulating the railroads to protect them from themselves was probably a mistake. It is a mistake we have continued for nearly a hundred years, and we may celebrate the centennial of the Interstate Commerce Commission before getting around to making some fundamental changes in that policy. If that is a precedent, it will probably be a very long time before we make any progress with all the recent regulation in the occupational health and safety area, the environmental area, and the product safety area.

Anyone who does not believe that reform will be this slow should consider a fact sheet distributed by the White House when it announced its regulatory reform proposals. Addressing former Congressman Rogers's concern about not focusing on the benefits, the White House press staff identified a "wide range of benefits" from regulation, specifically listing eight of them.

140

1. Workplace health standards, it says, are protecting more than 2½ million workers. But there are 100 million workers in this country. Two and a half million constitute a very small minority of them. The press release says nothing about any improvements in worker safety. Indeed, we are given no evidence that worker safety has been improved, and we have ample evidence that it has not. Clearly, the ability of the Occupational Safety and Health Administration to move aggressively is very seriously impeded by great uncertainty over the meaning of its enabling legislation. Perhaps some clarification will result from the lawsuit brought against OSHA's benzene standard, which is now being appealed to the Supreme Court. In the appellate court, OSHA was reversed for not having provided sufficient evidence of benefits to justify the enormous costs of this regulation.

2. Automobile safety devices are estimated to have saved 9,000 lives per year. One major economic study suggests, however, that there has been little, if any, saving of life. This is at best a debatable proposition.

3. Fuel economy standards, it says, yield savings in gasoline consumption of 1.3 million gallons per year. There is some question how much these standards are going to cost us; there is no doubt, however, that they are increasing the hold of General Motors on the market. In addition, the Commerce Department has estimated that the costs of the standards exceed the benefits by a rather wide margin.

4. Populated areas are said to have more protection against fires and so on. That benefit is one I cannot evaluate knowledgeably.

5. It is claimed that we are making real progress on water pollution. Here, even the environmentalists are beginning to have second thoughts as we continue to pour billions of dollars into a municipal grants program aimed at reducing pollutants that have little effect on human health.

6–8. The final three items advertised as "benefits of regulation" are *procedures* designed to help regulatory decision makers. A Regulatory Council has been established to prepare a Regulatory Calendar. The Regulatory Calendar has been prepared. A Regulatory Analysis Review Group has been formed to analyze the economic impact statements prepared by regulatory agencies. These are listed as "benefits of regulation."

If these eight "benefits" are all that can be advertised in response to the charge placed by Mr. Rogers and others after the White House has gone to its agencies for evidence of societal benefits, I fear that we are in trouble. If this is success, one would hate to encounter failure.

How do we reform this system? I believe that we have to go back to the individual statutes. To illustrate what is wrong, let us look at a paradigm, the so-called new source performance standards (NSPS) for coal-fired electrical utility boilers. The terminology is enough to put you to sleep, but it provides useful lessons.

What NSPS refers to, basically, is a decision which the Environmental Protection Agency has to make soon on what standards for sulfur dioxide and particulates to set for new power plants using coal. Back in 1977 there was a debate before Congress on revising the Clean Air Act. The existing regulations for protecting us from SO_2 were simply performance standards, specifying the number of pounds of SO_2 allowable per million B.t.u.s produced by an electrical utility plant. Coal miners in the midwestern part of the United States, particularly in Ohio, were concerned that these standards were going to displace them because their product was relatively high in sulfur. EPA and the Department of Energy testified before Congress in support of a proposal that would require all new electrical utilities to install the best available continuing emission control technology, regardless of the sulfur content of the coal being burned. This proposal essentially penalized low-sulfur western coal. The sensible thing to do would be to mine more such coal and less of the high-sulfur eastern coal. In fact, there was probably never any danger of sizable employment losses in the Midwest, and there is likely to be a substantial growth in coal mining anyway. What would have happened is that the growth increment would have come more from the West than from the Midwest. But the administration supported a very inefficient proposal for controlling SO_2 emissions in large part because of political pressures from Ohio coal miners and probably also because nobody understood what was going on.

After all, for the average congressman looking at the statute, it only says we should do the best we can, just use the best available technology. In the regulatory analysis process, however, one should analyze how much would it cost to do the most sensible thing, which is to put performance standards on public utilities or let them buy emission rights. But we cannot do that because the law now says utilities have to install that scrubbing equipment, regardless of how little sulfur is in the coal they use.

The result of the new provision of the law and of EPA's proposal to enforce it will be sulfur emissions that are higher than they would be with a slightly weaker standard, because the proposal is so onerous that the electrical utilities will postpone new plants and continue to belch sulfur from their old ones. In addition, it would add at least $1 billion a year to annual costs over and above what is necessary to get the same level of SO_2 emissions.

In that situation, what can the EPA do? What they should do is go back to Congress and say, "Look, we have an analysis that shows midwestern coal miners are not going to lose jobs. In fact, midwestern coal output will go up, even if we go to SO_2 performance standards. This is really a crazy law. We could save $1 billion a year. Let's repeal this section." What will happen instead, I suspect, is that the regulations will become more and more complicated as EPA tries to structure them in such a way as to minimize their adverse impact. The announcement of the initial proposed rule went on for 128 pages. EPA will probably double that in the final document.

Regulation becomes more and more complicated. People complain they do not understand it. They claim the regulators are doing us a disservice because of a political compromise reached during the legislative process. If we wish to change the policy, we can go back to a simple rule. It would be very easy for EPA to write a two-page document that says the new performance standard for electrical utilities is 0.8 or 0.9 pounds of SO_2 per million B.t.u.s and let utilities choose their own combination of coal and control equipment.

This example is but one of many needlessly complicated regulatory standards. We are going to have an expanding array of such regulation, regulation that will have to be modified, to be compartmentalized, to be divided and subdivided again to accommodate the political wishes of people in various parts of the country. It will become a mess.

To improve regulation, we should look at specific areas and begin to develop regulatory reform proposals in these areas. For example, we should certainly begin to get the DOE out of the regulation of gasoline prices, retailers' margins, refiners' margins, and of course out of crude oil regulation to alleviate the shortages of gasoline. That would allow us to eliminate the fuel economy standards, which are going to create tremendous costs, especially with the front loading that the Department of Transportation has so far been entertaining. It would get rid of the necessity for cartelizing the auto industry by asking them now to join forces with the government in developing a new generation of automobile engines, just a few years after the government dropped its case against the industry for conspiring to keep pollution control devices off the market.

In the environmental area, we should turn away from all the engineering standards that now make the bubble concept that Mr. Costle describes of relatively limited value. The bubble concept could be of considerable value, but there is not at present enough trade-off available because EPA sets the new source standard for every point source within a plant. This standard cannot be changed or traded.

I believe that we should change the primary ambient air standards, which Mr. Rogers had a great deal to do with as a congressman, requiring EPA to regulate air quality on the basis of the health of the most sensitive group of the population without regard to cost. In fact, since there are no demonstrated threshold effects in any of these air pollutants, one cannot set a standard that will protect the health of the most sensitive population except the standard of zero emissions. I am not a lawyer, of course, but I do not understand how these ambient air standards stand up in court.

In traditional areas of regulation, I certainly commend the administration for finally submitting a trucking deregulation bill. Clearly, the only reason we needed to regulate trucking was that it undermined our attempt to protect the railroads.

I would suggest very strongly that the administration support the deregulation of communications. There is no doubt that communications will be deregulated because the Federal Communications Commission, both legally and technologically, can no longer regulate it. It cannot stay ahead of the technology, and it cannot defend itself in the courts. The worst jobs in town must be those of the lawyers who defend the FCC in the court of appeals because they keep losing.

There is a variety of other things we could do. For instance, EPA and OSHA could both start moving toward economic incentives. At OSHA one would like to see an improvement in workers' compensation as a substitute for safety regulation, but not for health regulation. At EPA one would like to see firms penalized for polluting rather than for failing to install mandated equipment. This would be a far more efficient way of regulating. It would also give us the desired reduction in environmental pollution at a much lower cost.

The problem with regulation, if I may paraphrase Mr. Granquist, is that we knew what we wanted to do before we knew how to do it. It is interesting that he says this. This week marks the thirty-fifth anniversary of the Monte Casino assault by our armed forces in Italy. It seems the government is always capable of haste in decision making, whether it is the military or others. At Monte Casino we could not decide how to preserve the wonderful monastery while pursuing our strategic military objectives in the area. The various services argued about it for a long time. Finally, the Air Force came in and demolished the monastery. But the tactical support was not ready, and the assault served absolutely no strategic purpose. All it did was destroy a centuries-old monastery. Maybe this is the model of decision making our regulators are following. (Let me apologize to my friends who are regulators. I think most of them really are trying to quit.)

I disagree with Mr. Costle and Mr. Rogers that cost-benefit analysis is so difficult. I think what they are saying is that one does not want to write down what goes into a regulatory decision—one would rather make a decision on the basis of an unstated principle, a hunch or something. Take the ozone case in particular, the change from 0.08 parts per million to 0.12 parts per million of ozone. This is one of the few cases where even the Science Advisory Board broke with the EPA because there is very little evidence of health effects. The principal piece of evidence being cited over and over again is a study done in 1952 on the effects of photochemical smog on human beings—or the analysis of six healthy, exercising subjects in 1976. I would argue that we can estimate the cost of the oxidant standard within some confidence interval. We can probably also put a value on the benefits because ozone does not cause widespread death and suffering. Principally, as far as we know, it causes a reduction in pulmonary function, and it may aggravate emphysema. The uncertainty in the cost-benefit analysis is not in putting a value on the benefits or in calculating the costs; it is in establishing if there are any health benefits and exactly what they are. Not doing this analysis and writing it down obscures this fact from the public.

Bringing Back the
Regulatory Pendulum

Paul G. Rogers

Having had some responsibility while I was in Congress for passing laws on the subject of regulation, I have had to think about their rationale. When does government come in? When does government act? Why do we need laws and regulations? There are two answers.

The government is called upon by the people of this nation to take some action, first, when there has been a lack of action. When the private sector has not responded to a need, or when state and local governments have not responded, the pressures build for the federal government to try to solve the problem. The other situation where government is called upon to act is when there is excess action by the private sector or by citizens or even by government itself. This is the period we are now going through. The people of this nation are now calling on the federal government to stem some of the excess of its own regulation.

Previous administrations and previous congresses have proceeded to do something about lack of action—when no one was doing anything about the environment, when we had a lack of action in the health field, lack of action concerning safety conditions, lack of action for protection of consumers. Those congresses and those administrations responded with what we hoped were solutions. In those initial laws, of course, the goals set were to meet the problems that existed, and often the goals were set before we had the sophistication to detail how to accomplish the objective. That is the case with the environmental laws, for example. If we had not enacted these laws, we would have had little progress. If we had not started talking about cost containment in hospitals, there would be no voluntary program today. I can assure you of that.

The current administration, however, has come into office, probably more than any other, on the platform of doing something about too much regulation. I think some of the steps they are beginning to take against the excesses that have developed are very constructive. The administration is acting, as other contributors to this discussion have described. The president has already put out his executive orders. He is now trying to get those principles enacted into law to be effective across the entire regulatory field where the executive order does not now reach.

He is aided in this by the feeling in the nation and certainly among members of Congress. One hundred fifty bills have already been introduced. It will be one hundred fifty-one when Senator Kennedy introduces the legislation he discussed for a committee on the regulating process. I hope we will not have too many agencies set up to deregulate the regulators. That could be a problem. We might then have to have an agency to regulate the deregulators when they deregulate the regulators. We must be careful not to get too much regulation even as we go through the process of deregulation.

What we are actually seeing is the regulatory pendulum that has gone too far one way being brought back. The primary concerns of the basic laws are for the health and safety of the people. That is the underlying purpose of the Clean Air Act, the Occupational Safety and Health Act, the Toxic Substances Control Act, and so on. It is true that, although the law sets forth statements of economic considerations, there has not been enough emphasis during the formulation of regulations on the question of costs. The pendulum is now being brought back.

The danger is that if we come back too fast, we give such high priority to cost that we downplay the purpose of the law and the need for the law to protect health and safety. A proper balance has to be reached. That is not easy. It is very easy to specify costs. We can say what it will cost to put on environmental control devices, but our capacity to estimate the benefits is far behind our capacity to estimate the costs. I hope that in the administration's legislation or in any legislation that emerges there will be adequate requirements not to specify costs alone, but rather to apply as much emphasis, as much pressure, as much backup and technology to determining the benefits. Then one can make a proper judgment.

Industry is ready for this. It was difficult for industry initially to accept environmental controls, but now they accept them as a way of doing business. Industry now understands the importance of protecting the Love Canal, and there are many such examples. Industry is very much concerned, but they want to do these things in the most economical way, as do the government and the people. This is the movement now.

There are some dangers that we ought to keep in mind in moving too rapidly in this change. These include, first, the difficulty of determining benefits. If we go to a certain point in cleaning up NO_2 from automobiles, which is expensive, how do we balance that cost against improving the health of 25 million children and the elderly? That health improvement is difficult to articulate in a dollars-and-cents way. We need to try to improve our ability to do that.

Second, most of the cost-benefit analyses we see are generated by those whose costs would be affected by the regulations. They do not bring out the benefits. Maybe there ought to be an obligation in the law that those who come forth with the costs must also present the facts on the corresponding benefits.

Another danger we have to keep in mind is that there is a false precision about cost-benefit analyses that tends to discount or negate the necessary value judgments, the ethical and moral judgments that a legislative body simply must make. Legislation is not simply a matter of totaling up costs and benefits on a calculator. That is not the way laws are made, and that is something we have to remember.

Fourth, the administration will have to be very careful, as we get deeper into this cost-benefit analysis, not to create an institutional polarization within the executive branch. Such a rift is already beginning to develop between the cost-generating agencies and the cost-controlling watchdogs. There are some, in fact, who feel that the watchdogs ought to be treated like outside people, not even a part of the government. When the watchdogs bark, these groups say it ought not to be on an ex parte basis. This issue will have to be faced. Probably the best way to deal with the polarization is to have the cost analysis people also come in with the benefits, so that they present a balanced judgment that people can use to make decisions.

Our basic need, really, is just for a proper balance, a reasonable administration, bringing back the pendulum, trying to cut off the excesses, but still taking action about the needs that exist. By giving proper attention and properly stressing benefits as well as costs, we can come to intelligent judgments. All of us believe that economic costs should certainly be a major consideration in regulatory government. But it must be in the context of a balanced judgment so that we accomplish our goals and not let the pendulum swing too far one way or the other.

Summary of Discussion

In the discussion that followed the presentations on the administration's regulatory reform initiatives, Mr. Crandall's attack on the regulators provoked a vigorous defense by administration spokesmen and Mr. Rogers. To the suggestion that forcing negligent employers to pay more for workers' compensation would cut down on injuries, Mr. Rogers responded that "in this nation we are beyond having to say 'Let's don't do anything until we have all the dead bodies.' The point of environmental law and of health laws is prevention."

Mr. Costle offered a lengthy rebuttal to Mr. Crandall. He challenged the contention that data did not support some of the EPA's decisions, saying that scientists were able to reach enough of a consensus to make regulatory decisions rational. At the same time, he admitted that regulators of the environment, health, and safety were operating on the "frontiers of science." The EPA, Mr. Costle said, is regularly put in the position of asking itself, What would a reasonably prudent person do in the face of uncertainty? And he answered his own question: "We have no choice as a society unless we want to put blinders on and think the future is really today. We have no choice but to take some fairly stiff, prudent preventive measures. We have to accept the fact that we will be operating without the sure comfort of having pinned everything down, dotted all the i's, and crossed all the t's of what we have to work on. But it would be irresponsible not to take action."

A questioner from the floor asked whether it would not be more efficient to ensure that companies knew they would suffer if they were responsible for an environmental or safety disaster than to impose detailed regulation. If Hooker Chemical Co. had known it might have to pay millions of dollars to clean up the Love Canal in upstate New York, would it not have invested the few hundreds of thousands of dollars needed to prevent the chemical leaks in the first place?

"They were aware of the dangers, and they still did it," Mr. Rogers replied. Mr. Costle said that in "an alarming number of cases" the parties responsible for environmental damages did not have enough money to clean them up. Regulation was needed to ensure that the

149

damage did not occur in the first place. Mr. Costle admitted, however, that the government does not have all the answers. "Congress has in the last fifteen years rewritten the basic social charter between corporate America and the rest of America. We are adjusting to that, figuring out how to work with it effectively and efficiently." Added Mr. Eads, "The statutes themselves, for historical reasons or because people did not know better, are inconsistent in many cases. They mandate different results."

Our best approach, Mr. Eads suggests, is to "get away from treating regulation with a sense of moral outrage and recognize it for what it is—a way of changing the incentive structure of doing business, putting the government into private decision making. We must treat it as a management problem."

Part
Eight

Overview and Summary

Reforms in Procedure, Structure, Personnel, and Substance

Lloyd N. Cutler

Whenever I try to summarize a program like this, I think with envy of the British solicitor with whom I shared a platform once on a program dealing with the antitrust laws of Europe and the United States. He stood up and said, "My assignment is to describe to you the antitrust laws of Britain, Germany, and France." He continued, "I can do it in three sentences. In Britain everything that is not expressly forbidden is allowed. In Germany everything that is not expressly allowed is forbidden. In France everything is forbidden but almost anything can be arranged." Then he sat down. That perhaps is what I should do here, but I will try instead to summarize the debate so far and then add a few comments of my own.

The best departure point is Mr. Breyer's division of the various regulatory reform initiatives into four categories. These are the same categories that appear in the report from the American Bar Association Commission on Law and Economy, to which both Mr. Breyer and I contributed. He divided the various suggestions and criticisms into the four fields of procedure, structure, personnel, and substance. Of course, there are some current initiatives, such as the president's intervention in regulatory matters and the legislative veto, that seem to partake of all four. They may need a separate heading that we could call balance or accountability. I notice that "balance" has been the key word in this conference.

Of course, there is some merit in all these proposals. There is enough wrong with regulation that almost anything that is proposed is probably going to do some good. Some of the suggestions, though, work at cross-purposes. A good illustration is the emphasis placed in the administration's proposals on the simplification and speeding up of regulatory procedures—coupled with provisions for increasing funds for public participation and for those who would represent additional interest groups that somehow have not managed to get to the table yet and in some cases causing the extension, rather than the contraction, of the time of comment.

In the procedural category, I tend to share Mr. Breyer's view that there is not very much that can usefully be done, and not much was discussed in this conference. Certainly, deadlines, the so-called new simplified procedures, and so on would be valuable. A move away from trying everything on the record and from having cross-examination would also be worthwhile.

Sunset, on the other hand, I have doubts about. I do not see how it could do much harm, and it probably would have a prophylactic effect on the agencies to have a deadline every now and then at which they have to justify what they have been doing. Still, the generations remain to be born who will actually witness the departure of an agency into the sunset as a result of the action or inaction of Congress. We have now had the first two experiences with statutes providing sunset deadlines that have come and gone. The first—and I would think a rather good case could have been made against this agency—was the Consumer Product Safety Commission. It, of course, is being permitted to continue, as is the second, the Commodities Futures Trading Commission. In both cases Congress did nothing, and even the fact that a sunset deadline had come and gone has received virtually no notice, even on programs like this.

Impact statements, cost-benefit analyses, and regulatory analyses are certainly well worth doing, and in some ways they relate more to substance than to procedures. A more radical suggestion might be just to close the law schools. A few references were made to all the lawyers who mess things up. Japan, with 100 million people, has only 10,000 lawyers—one for every 10,000 people. Europe averages about one for every 35,000 people, even in Britain, the home of due process. We have 460,000 lawyers. That is one for every 500 people in the United States. In Washington, D.C., and its environs, the ratio is about one to every 80. In fact, I once made a calculation that one in every 30 people gainfully employed in the Washington area is a lawyer.

That, of course, is a cut-off-your-foot solution, but it does tell us something. Regulatory problems are not the fault of the lawyers, of course. What the fact does show is that we in the United States have a greater faith in laws and regulations as a solution to social problems, and in litigation as a means of enforcing laws, than any country on earth. That is why the only great growth industry or profession in this country over the last decade or so has been the lawyers. Right behind them, of course, and coming up strong are the economists.

Structure, it seems to me, is hardly worth discussing, just as Mr. Breyer said. The only real issue there is the dichotomy between the independent agencies and the executive branch agencies. I defy anyone to come up with a coherent principle to explain why some agencies are made independent in their enabling statutes while others are placed under the president's authority.

As to personnel, I also agree with the comments that have been made, although there have been only a few. The notion that it would all be better if we just had better members on the agencies and the commissions is not going to take us very far. We should note that with the coming of Alfred Kahn to the Civil Aeronautics Board, he and his colleagues on the board were able to accomplish, without the benefit of the new deregulation statute, most of the results that that statute was intended to achieve. It could have been done all along if the members of the CAB had been so disposed and if they had had, of course, the accumulated wisdom that came out of the evidence Mr. Breyer developed about how poorly rate and entry control was working in air transportation.

With the first three categories eliminated as sources of promising changes, we come to substance. It is a good thing that this conference spent most of its time on this type of reform. It is tremendously important, certainly, that more analyses like those that led to the reform of the CAB be initiated. Senator Kennedy's program, it seems to me, is highly desirable. I agree with the suggestions made that very high on the agenda should be an analysis of the entire energy field and also of our health and safety regulations. The latter is to me the biggest, most important regulatory problem of all. I have a feeling, though, that while this kind of analysis may lead economists and political scientists to a better understanding of what kind of regulation or input of government influence would be the most effective, it will have to be tempered by the common characteristic shared by most command-and-control health and safety regulation today—that whether it is the least restrictive economically is far less important than whether it is the least intrusive politically.

For almost any given problem, say, highway safety or fuel economy, the simplest solution by far, other than the market solution of letting prices go up, would be direct regulation of the driver. Such an approach would impose more stringent penalties for drunken driving, which probably accounts for more accidents than any other single cause. It would mean enforcing the 55-mile-per-hour speed limit. It would mean the return to a semimarket solution, much higher taxes on gasoline. Every one of these measures imposes a cost, however, either a money cost or an inconvenience cost, directly on a voter or a consumer, and they are therefore politically unacceptable. It is much easier to impose hidden costs, even though we all know that they are going to be borne ultimately by the same consumers. It is easier to impose the direct requirements on manufacturers who, after a lot of moaning and groaning, will finally succumb, against whom the government can enforce its directives much more easily, and who in turn will, as they always do, pass on the costs to the same ultimate public.

But the public is much more willing to accept hidden costs. The best possible illustration of that is that no one would pay personally for an emission control device if it were offered on that basis. The device increases gasoline consumption and decreases performance. People would not pay for it if they had a choice—and did not when they did have a choice. Yet we are perfectly willing to have a law that will enable the Environmental Protection Agency to impose emission control standards on manufacturers who will in turn impose those costs on us in a hidden way. That is one of the great dilemmas of regulation and one of the realities that the economists and lawyers and businessmen as well as politicians have to recognize. The politicians have probably known it all along.

The second of the substantive proposals relates to the problem of balance, how we balance out the effects of regulation. I will come back to that in a moment. The third, which Mr. Dunlop deals with, is the matter of cost-benefit analysis. I would like to add one comment on that.

Although it may be the first time, I agree with something Mr. Green said. I think he was quoting Congressman John Moss when he said the most important thing about a cost-benefit analysis is who prepared it. I do not mean what he meant—if industry prepared it, we should mistrust it. In everything industry prepares, it naturally stresses its side of a controversial issue, and there will be something else prepared by a public interest group or an agency. Those will offset each other. It is a fact, though, and it is one of the problems of cost-benefit analysis that, so far as I know, no agency has ever prepared a cost-benefit analysis and concluded that the costs of what it wanted to do outweighed the benefits. That is important because the agency is the decision maker. A single-mission agency has an invariable tendency to decide in favor of the mission Congress gave it.

Let me return to the subject of balance. We know today that we have many competing and conflicting social goals that we want government to promote. Even in a country as rich as this, we cannot possibly accomplish every one of those goals to its fullest measure at the same time. I need only mention the trade-off between energy self-sufficiency and the environment to show how obvious that is. Yet we have given each of these goals to a different single-mission agency. There are very few methods by which the competing and conflicting nature of the missions of those agencies can be reconciled.

156

Mr. Kristol made a point that I would like to develop a bit further. He referred to how much more efficient and effective regulation was in Europe, even though it is largely conducted by socialist governments. He explained that those socialists have to form governments and are held responsible for what they do, and therefore they regulate more effectively and are more conscious of the overall balance of what they are trying to do.

He could have elaborated that point into what I see as the biggest single problem we have in regulation—and it is not limited to regulation. It is that no one forms a government in this country and is held accountable for the results of that government. In every country in Europe that I know of, every regulatory agency—and they have just as many as we do—is directly under the control of the cabinet. The cabinet, of course, is formed by the majority of the legislature. Every five years, and sometimes more often, the voters or the legislature itself rejects that particular government, and it leaves office. But that government is accountable for everything that happens while it is in office. How many congressmen in this country, critical as they are of regulation, recognize that they are responsible for the laws under which these regulations are being issued? They do not. In the last election, both the incumbent president, Mr. Ford, and the challenger, Mr. Carter, ran against the bureaucracy without any sense in the world that they were accountable for what the bureaucracy was doing.

The single-mindedness of particular agencies and interest groups, which we have all talked about, is best illustrated by the irony of the National Environmental Protection Act (NEPA) as contrasted with EPA. NEPA said to every agency, "Before you carry out your particular mission, whether it is licensing offshore oil wells or lending money to foreign governments or whatever else, remember the environment. Consider the impact on the environment and make sure that what you do has taken account of the environment as another goal of government." When the EPA's enabling legislation was passed, however, it became the position of environmentalists and of Mr. Costle, despite what he says about cost-benefit analysis, that EPA is constrained by law to consider only the health needs of the country and is not allowed to take other goals, such as inflation, employment, economic growth, or energy impacts, into account. That is what happens with single-mission agencies.

The only solution to that problem I know of—I have written about this, and the ABA commission has made such a proposal—is to let the president exercise control over the agencies, at least those within the executive branch, so as to supply the necessary balance. And by "the president," I mean of course the Charles Schultzes and George Eadses and others who, even though they are also at least temporarily bureaucrats, are also bureaucrats thinking from an overall point of view rather than a single-mission point of view. There are some serious procedural problems to presidential intervention—when it should be done, under what circumstances, on or off the record. All of them can be solved. It is important that we recognize the need for some sort of balance and that only the president can possibly supply it. We must set appropriate procedures by which he and his assistants can act.

Setting Priorities
in Government Regulation

John T. Dunlop

Mr. Cutler told me this morning that he had spent the weekend in Alaska. I spent the weekend reading fifty term papers dealing with business and government and regulation. Compared with five years ago, the graduate students in the Kennedy School, the Harvard Business School, and the Faculty of Arts and Sciences are very much interested in this range of problems. They have also shifted their views, as is often the case among the young, from very strong support five years ago for government regulation to an enormous skepticism and cynicism today.

One of these papers dealt with the regulation of upholstered furniture flammability by the Consumer Product Safety Commission; another with the requirement in the Toxic Substances Control Act for premanufacturing notification; another with the regulation of television advertising for children; another with accounting standards of gas and oil firms; and still others with national security, export control, automobile bumper regulations, the Ethics in Government Act of 1978, the saccharin problem, and so on and on. Discussions like these are quite useful as long as we keep them focused on facts. If we can prepare in our universities and other research institutions careful, detailed case studies of particular regulatory programs—how they came to be, what was intended, how other factors worked out, the measurement of results to the best of our knowledge—our society will over the course of five to ten years have a more dispassionate approach to these problems than the strongly political perspective that has predominated in the past. This process of careful, critical review is now well under way in educational institutions.

I share Mr. Cutler's general view that global schemes to reform regulation are dubious. I am very much a bits-and-pieces person in this matter; I do not think that such approaches as sunset laws or the congressional veto will take us very far. What is of central importance, from my perspective, is a certain point of view. Everyone may not agree with it, but it was the perspective that in 1975 led me to write for my staff a document entitled "The Limits of Legal Compulsion: What You Can Do with a Piece of Paper and What You Can't."

Our present situation overall is one in which the government has vastly more on its regulatory agenda than it can ever deliver. As a result, governmental processes are often bogged down in quagmires of delay and litigation, creating serious uncertainty problems, and people are becoming increasingly disillusioned about those processes. We must approach problems in the regulatory area with a stronger sense of the need to establish priorities. What are the five things that an agency should be doing? Or what are the most important two or three things in this area and in that area? We must move away from the notion that every problem that can be addressed under a statute should be aggressively pursued by an agency.

I recognize that formal analysis might suggest that one should push the limits of regulation to the point where at the margin the social gains are equal to costs, as best we can measure them, but that is dead wrong. We do not in the private sector push investment to the point where the marginal rate of return is equal to the interest rate, as the theory suggests. What we do in our private enterprises, in our personal lives, and in our nonprofit institutions is to pick out a few key things to do and concentrate on them. We should also proceed this way in the regulatory field. We need to specify the three or four—the limited number—of key things that need to be done and concentrate on them. The cost-benefit framework, important as it is, is not a formula to determine in some automatic way at the margin which things to do and which not to do.

The perspective that I am proposing is related to a broader philosophical problem that confronts the society. All our institutions have increasingly and in various contexts been called upon to do things that they are not well suited to do, and they make a mess out of trying. Our universities, for instance, have gone through a period in which some students and faculty members thought of them as some kind of all-purpose reform institutions with a mission in society to "straighten things out." Universities are fairly good at training people and at pursuing research. They are not very good at reforming society, and they should stay out of that business. Individual professors, of course, should be free to speak their minds in keeping with our traditions; that is not my point. I am saying that by taking on missions that as institutions they were never intended for and are not suited for, the universities have experienced enormous costs in terms of public perceptions of their performance.

Another example is the labor movement. We have had generations of intellectuals in this country who have tried to pervert the labor movement by transforming it into something it did not wish to be. It has historically wished to be primarily an agency for bargaining and also a lobbying organization for various social programs that have broad consensus within the membership. Yet some intellectuals and others have sought to divert the movement from those historical, long-term objectives toward some kind of all-purpose mission to reform society and, in general, to end social injustice. Labor unions were not formed for these purposes, these were not the primary goals of the membership, and consequently they could not perform this role well.

Similarly, we need to have a more limited view of what government is capable of doing. I deeply admire government, and I have frequently worked with it, but it can help with only a limited number of problems. When it takes on an unlimited agenda of tasks, pushing social reform to the limits under the kinds of general legislation that have been enacted, it will certainly fall into a quagmire, and this will have a very serious adverse impact. That is my assessment of our situation, and I believe that this viewpoint on limiting our objectives is increasingly being recognized.

I would also like to make some observations about developing and applying regulations. I believe that it is possible in many regulatory areas to introduce a much greater degree of negotiation to create consensus, to promote agreement instead of litigation. These comments are not critical of lawyers because I know many lawyers who are very good at negotiations. I tell my economics students at the university that most economics courses are about markets. These students are not, I am afraid, admirers of markets. Our society has become increasingly distrustful of markets, whether we deal with markets in international trade, with labor markets, or with product markets. Elementary economics tells us about markets, but I emphasize that many of society's problems today are being settled by negotiations. That is what I do with much of my time—mediate, negotiate. Professional lawyers who are interested in changing problems into negotiations are people whom I greatly admire.

There are any number of ways to develop in the regulatory arena a higher degree of voluntarism and negotiation and therefore, in my judgment, consent to live with the regulations. I devoutly believe that there is almost nothing you can compel the American people to do, but there is almost no end to the things you can persuade them to do. That should be written on the walls of people who run regulatory agencies.

As an example, consider the agreement signed with the consent of the Occupational Safety and Health Administration by building trades people and large contractors in California. As an experiment under a state plan approved by OSHA, it provides that OSHA will not make the normal on-site investigations on every project for nonserious problems. It will turn that responsibility completely over to the parties, who will make systematic investigations with two of their own representatives on each side. They will submit a report, the report will be reviewed, and so on. The experiment is now in its fifth month, and it seems to be working very well in terms of saving staff time and in terms of practicality. This is the kind of approach we should experiment with.

The relevance and contribution of data sets have been a continuing issue in the regulatory reform debate. The problem with data sets is not merely one of scientific objectivity; it is also very much a matter of acceptability, of confidence in how they are developed and interpreted, and of willingness to deal with them. Hence the role of the parties in the development of data sets is very important, and this is sometimes a difficult role. Mr. Cutler has been involved in a proposal to provide for the development of a comprehensive data set for health and safety and environmental regulations. Industry, labor, and other groups that are affected by those regulations would have a degree of confidence in the data sets that they do not now have. An example comes from the meat-cutting area. My friends in the retail food industry went to a university and put up $600,000 or $700,000 to have studies made on the health effects of polyvinyl chloride wrappings. They then discussed proposed standards and data sets to be used in the regulatory process.

It may be that the perspectives and approaches that I have suggested will turn out not to be equally and uniformly applicable in every case. But until attitudes in society are permeated to a greater degree by some of these perspectives on government regulation and how it is carried out, we run the danger of becoming hopelessly bogged down and of creating a general reaction against many policies that would in principle be constructive and well worth pursuing.

A NOTE ON THE BOOK

The typeface used for the text of this book is Times Roman, designed by Stanley Morison. The type was set by Foto-Typesetters Incorporated, of Baltimore, Maryland. Braun-Brumfield, Inc., of Ann Arbor, Michigan, printed and bound the book, using paper manufactured by the S. D. Warren Company. Cover and format were designed by Pat Taylor.

The manuscript was edited by Janet Marantz and by Gertrude Kaplan, of the AEI Publications staff.

SELECTED AEI PUBLICATIONS

Regulation: The AEI Journal on Government and Society, published bi-monthly (one year, $12; two years, $22; single copy, $2.50)

A Conversation with Douglas Costle (24 pp., $2.25)

Perspectives on Postal Service Issues, Roger Sherman, ed. (228 pp., paper $7.25, cloth $10.25)

A Conversation with Commissioner Eleanor Holmes Norton (23 pp., $2.25)

Vehicle Safety Inspection Systems: How Effective? W. Mark Crain (70 pp., $4.25)

U.S. Industry in Trouble: What Is the Government's Responsibility? Peter Hackes, mod. (18 pp., $3.75)

Regulatory Reform in Air Cargo Transportation, Lucile Sheppard Keyes (56 pp., $4.25)

Reducing Risks to Life: Measurement of the Benefits, Martin J. Bailey (66 pp., $4.25)

A Conversation with Michael Pertschuk (26 pp., $3.25)

Prices subject to change without notice.

AEI ASSOCIATES PROGRAM

The American Enterprise Institute invites your participation in the competition of ideas through its AEI Associates Program. This program has two objectives:

The first is to broaden the distribution of AEI studies, conferences, forums, and reviews, and thereby to extend public familiarity with the issues. AEI Associates receive regular information on AEI research and programs, and they can order publications and cassettes at a savings.

The second objective is to increase the research activity of the American Enterprise Institute and the dissemination of its published materials to policy makers, the academic community, journalists, and others who help shape public attitudes. Your contribution, which in most cases is partly tax deductible, will help ensure that decision makers have the benefit of scholarly research on the practical options to be considered before programs are formulated. The issues studied by AEI include:

- Defense Policy
- Economic Policy
- Energy Policy
- Foreign Policy
- Government Regulation
- Health Policy
- Legal Policy
- Political and Social Processes
- Social Security and Retirement Policy
- Tax Policy

For more information, write to:
AMERICAN ENTERPRISE INSTITUTE
1150 Seventeenth Street, N.W.
Washington, D.C. 20036